THE MILK SOY PROTEIN INTOLERANCE (MSPI)

THE MILK SOY PROTEIN INTOLERANCE (MSPI)

GUIDEBOOK / COOKBOOK

TAMARA FIELD

authorHOUSE®

AuthorHouse™ LLC
1663 Liberty Drive
Bloomington, IN 47403
www.authorhouse.com
Phone: 1-800-839-8640

This book contains information and experiences of this author and is meant to be a resource, and not a nutritional guide, and does should not medical advice. You should always read nutritional labels thoroughly and carefully. Recipes and product information at the time of this writing is subject to change as manufacturing and ingredient availability shifts.

2nd Edition, 2013

Published by AuthorHouse   12/12/2013

ISBN: 978-1-4918-3809-9 (sc)
ISBN: 978-1-4918-3808-2 (e)

Library of Congress Control Number: 2013921587

Any people depicted in stock imagery provided by Thinkstock are models, and such images are being used for illustrative purposes only.
Certain stock imagery © Thinkstock.

This book is printed on acid-free paper.

Because of the dynamic nature of the Internet, any web addresses or links contained in this book may have changed since publication and may no longer be valid. The views expressed in this work are solely those of the author and do not necessarily reflect the views of the publisher, and the publisher hereby disclaims any responsibility for them.

CONTENTS

DEDICATION

To all my boys . . . my husband, Larry for your support, and encouragement. To Max and Nate, who at 15 and 17, are so far from the infants I first wrote about. I am so proud of you both and love you each so dearly.

FOREWORD

Milk Soy Protein Intolerance is commonly acknowledged and diagnosed by both pediatricians and family physicians. In the medical field this occurrence is also known as eosinophilic gastroenteritis. MSPI is diagnosed by the history of an infant with irritability (colic-like behavior), poor growth, abnormal stools; some of which visibly show blood. Confirmation of the diagnosis is often made by a biopsy of the intestinal tissue showing an increased amount of eosinophilic cells, eroded intestinal villi, and hemorrhagic tissue. An increase in the level of eosinophilic cells may also correlate with an allergic response of the intestinal tissues due to the introduction of an allergic compound. Many physicians request that parents alter the infant's formula or the mother's diet (for breastfed infants) prior to having a gastroenterologist perform an invasive  biopsy, then if the symptoms diminish, or even cease, the diagnosis of MSPI is assumed.

Both formula-fed and breast-fed infants can develop an intolerance to cow's milk protein and also soy protein. For infants fed with formula it is easy to change to a different formula, but more specialized formulas are more expensive. For many families the cost of these formulas are prohibitive. For an infant who is breastfed the mother's diet must be altered to avoid milk and soy proteins in order to continue breastfeeding. This approach is certainly a less costly solution to the dietary demands of an MSPI infant.

As a pediatrician who suspects MSPI, I first advise the breastfeeding mother to eliminate all dairy products from her diet, then if the infant=s symptoms decrease I advise the mother to continue with the dietary restrictions. If these measures help, but the infant is still fussy, irritable, or having blood streaked stools, then I also suggest removing soy products from the mother's diet. To date, I have had only one handout to give to mothers on the dietary restrictions for MSPI. This consisted of a list of the following foods: plain fruit, vegetables, meats, a certain type of french bread, and a list of ingredients to be avoided on the MSPI diet. All packaged or processed items with milk or soy proteins must be eliminated. I cannot imagine what hope I offered to these mothers as I sent them out of my office.

This book offers a realistic approach to MSPI and the breastfeeding mother's dietary restrictions. This guidebook and cookbook goes beyond offering the standard information about MSPI, it offers guidance on products, manufacturers, and foods or products that may be substituted for those commonly used items that must be avoided on this diet. In addition, it offers support and knowledge to the mother who must make the immediate and drastic changes necessary in her diet to continue breastfeeding her infant and easing the symptoms of MSPI.

Monique L. Macklem, M.D.

Dr. Macklem is a Fellow of the American Academy of Pediatricians and also an Associate Professor of Pediatrics at Creighton University in Omaha.

INTRODUCTION

I first heard of Milk Soy Protein Intolerance (MSPI) in January of 1997 at the office of a Pediatric Gastroenterologist who had just performed a procto-sigmoidoscopy and biopsy on my 7 week old son. He told me that Max's digestive problem was MSPI and that it would be much easier for me if I stopped breastfeeding now and put him on a special formula. Of course, at that moment my head was spinning; I had finally found out the reason my son had been screaming the first 7 weeks of his life and though I wanted to continue breastfeeding I did not want to cause him anymore pain. The Doctor told me that there was a diet I could follow to continue breastfeeding, but that it was very difficult to follow. Wanting to make the best choice for my son I stopped breast-feeding that day and started him on formula.

In retrospect, the physician was right, even though I regret that I did not continue breastfeeding, with the demands of a new infant, and trying to figure out a complicated diet, would have been completely overwhelming. I knew though, that if I had any more children, I would try any diet possible in order to breastfeed. So, during the first few months of my pregnancy with my second son, Nate, I began preparing for the MSPI diet.

Determined that I would not lack for good things to eat, and that I <u>would</u> find chocolate that was acceptable on this diet, I started shopping. Little by little, I found many alternatives for the food I previously enjoyed (the only exception being cheese!). I found chocolate, cake, brownies, casseroles, pasta, rice milk, rice, breads, fast food, eating out, and so much more, even a substitute for ice cream! It just took a lot of planning and a bit of ingenuity.

Now, in 2013, as I write this second edition, there are so many great alternatives for dairy, even cheese, which was not the case in 2001. I have added many new recipes and edited many of the old recipes with some new ingredients and measurements. In addition, there are updated products, product lists, resources and recipes.

At this time in my life, I am far removed from the infant days, but I will never forget the desperation I felt with my first son and how I would do absolutely anything to help him feel better. I am so blessed now to have such a healthy, happy children.

The impetus for this edition was simple, the first publisher I had went out of business and shortly after hearing that news, I found out from many of the local Lactation Specialists that there were no more books available, so the direction was clear.

As mentioned in the previous edition, my goal in writing this book is to be of help the women who is handed a list of ingredients and told to "stay on this diet and you can keep breastfeeding" or "avoid all milk and soy products." Once you start reading food labels you will wonder if there is any food that you can eat. The food substitutions guide will give you quick ideas to get started and then you can expand into other products and recipes at your own pace and there are so many more options at the time of this printing.

I stayed on the MSPI diet strictly for over a year, and I still find myself looking for alternatives to dairy and soy. At a time when much is questioned of what we add to our foods or feed to our animals in order to make their meat and dairy products "better," many people are turning away from animal products, whether dairy or meat, and trying to figure out reasonable alternatives. This guidebook/cookbook will help you avoid dairy and soy products for whatever reason you are doing so and enjoy it.

INGREDIENTS TO AVOID ON THE MILK SOY PROTEIN INTOLERANCE DIET

Milk products:

butter
casein/caseinate
condensed milk
cream, half and half
cottage cheese/curd
evaporated milk
ghee
lactalbumin/lactoglobulin
lactose/lactulose
milk/milk solids/milk protein
milk chocolate (plus most other chocolates)
nonfat dry milk
whey, whey protein

Soy products:

edamame
miso
soy beans
soy flour
soy protein isolate
soy caseinate
textured or hydrolyzed vegetable protein (tvp or hvp)
soy sauce
tamari sauce
tempeh
tofu
vegetable gum
*soy oil is okay, as is soy lecithin; they are fats.

FOOD SUBSTITUTIONS

While there is much it seems that you cannot eat on this diet, there are many things out there that you can use as substitutions. You simply must know where to look. This section will go through each food group and give useful food substitutions, where they exist, for the foods you are giving up. If you get home from shopping and notice that you bought a product that contains one of the "forbidden" ingredients take it back. This means you must keep your receipts. The stores I shopped at were very accommodating in refunding money or exchanging products for me when I explained the problem.

IMPORTANT—YOU MUST ALWAYS READ LABELS CAREFULLY. Products may change and it is easy to miss ingredients that should be avoided and products are always subject to change.

Dairy—there are not any dairy products that are suitable on this diet, because they all contain milk protein, but there are many alternatives.

Alternative Milks—comparison table. There are so many out there that the only way to figure out which one is the right for you, is to taste them all.

Alternative Milk Comparison (serving size 1 cup)

	Coconut	Almond	Rice	Hemp	Flax	Oat	Hazelnut
Calories	80	60	120	110	50	130	110
Fat	5 g	2.5 g	2.5 g	6 g	2.5 g	2.5	3.5
Carbs	0.8 g	0.6 g	23 g	12 g	1.0 g	24	18
Protein	1 g	1 g	1 g	2 g	0 g	4	2
Calcium	45%	45%	30%	0%	30%	35%	30%

Calcium % daily value

Almond milk—Dark Chocolate is my favorite. It is available in enriched as well and is available in original, vanilla, sweetened, unsweetened, etc.

Coconut milk—love this! It is good in coffee, straight, and in recipes and comes in many flavors. I even found Coconut Pumpkin flavor milk for fall.

Rice milk—still available in most supermarkets, thinner in texture and body. Comes in several different flavors.

Oat milk—again available in original, vanilla and chocolate, but often a bit harder to find.

Hemp, Flax, and Hazelnut milk—are options, but aren't as easy to find.

The major manufacturers are Silk, Almond Breeze (Blue Diamond), and Almond Dream (Rice Dream). There is a new blend on the market from Califia Farms; Almond Milk Latte, Espresso and Mocha, plus an almond coconut blend—these are very good.

Cream/Creamer—**So Delicious** makes some great coffee creamers. Beware of "non-dairy" or "lactose-free" creamers, whether liquid or powdered, they often contain soy protein, (if they are truly "non-dairy"), and also often contain caseinate.

Butter—**Fleischmann's** unsalted stick margarine is great for baking and cooking.

Earth's Balance spreads and stick margarine. This is really good. It is available in it's many varieties in most supermarkets, and is still my pick for margarine (over butter-really) today. They sell other spreads, nut butters and shortenings some are soy-based, but most are milk/soy protein free. I have tried the shortening in cookies, and didn't care for the taste, the margarine is much better for baking.

Crisco—regular or butter flavor, are also useful for baking. You should use a little less crisco than the amount butter or margarine that is called for.

Cheese—there is finally substitute for cheese without caseinate—**Daiya** and **Go Cheese.** Daiya "cheese" alternative is made from only vegetable products. It is pretty good in recipes, but I am not a fan of it plain. You really have to try a few and choose which one you like, if any. For that reason, I did not incorporate it into many recipes; it was better without. I did like the cheddar style shreds in burritos, eggs or baked dishes. My best advice is to try a few flavors and see what you like.

The other option is Nutritional yeast flakes, you can sprinkle them on pastas, popcorn and eggs for a parmesan taste. Again, try it, see what you like.

*What about Goat's milk? Though goat milk used to be used for many babies (I was one!) who had digestive disturbances that could not be diagnosed and some babies tolerated it; the protein in cow's milk and goat's milk are very similar, so it is not generally recommended as an alternative.

Yogurt—there are now almond regular and greek, and coconut milk varieties. They are good and also nice substitutes in baking.

Sour cream—no substitute, really. I have tried to sour rice milk, and that didn't work and even "non-dairy" or "lactose-free" sour cream most likely contains either caseinate, whey, or soy protein. If you use sour cream in mexican cooking, try substituting guacamole instead. A plain almond or coconut yogurt would be the closest substitute.

Eggs—eggs are not a dairy product (thought they are often referred to as dairy), you may eat eggs and also most egg substitutes.

Spreads/Fats

Oil—nearly any oil can be used except soy. Read labels carefully on <u>flavored</u> oils, some have added milk products to imitate a "buttery" taste.

Peanut Butter—many popular commercial brands of peanut butter contain soy protein. Try a "natural" peanut butter, or your grocery chains brand.

Mayonnaise—Regular or "lite" varieties of mayonnaise should be okay. In all my checks of both popular and food chain varieties I failed to find one that listed either milk or soy products. There are alternative versions such as vegannaise that are also very good. Earth Balance makes a good "mayonnaise" spread.

Mustard—most varieties are acceptable.

Brown Sauces—such as soy, tamari, worchestershire, hoisin and brown sauce: these all contain soy. If it is brown in color, it most likely contains soy, so read the label carefully.

Ketchup, **Barbeque sauces**—many varieties are acceptable.

Salsa and Picante Sauces—most are acceptable. A fresh Pico de gallo is always a good alternative.

Salad Dressings—look for non-creamy varieties here, such as italian, or vinaigrettes. You must be careful to check for parmesan cheese in some italian brands. Kraft's Good Seasons Italian, Zesty Italian and Herb Garlic powdered dressing mixes are milk/soy protein free as are many olive oil based dressings.

Hummus—Great spread on breads, for sandwiches or used as a dip. You can find hummus in many flavors in the gourmet or cheese section of most stores. Athenos, Sabra and Melissa's are common brands, you just have to be careful to avoid those with cheese, such as feta, or parmesan.

Dips—most commercially packaged dips contain milk products such as sour cream, milk or whey. Hummus, salsa, bean and guacamole dips are good substitutes for that creamy craving. Guacamole is often best made from scratch as pre-packaged varieties can contain milk products for added creaminess.

Snacks\Desserts

Crackers—There are a few popular brands of crackers that at this printing do not contain any forbidden products: Nabisco's Triscuit and Wheat Thins, Lavosh and Carr's Water Crackers are a few. Some brands of crackers may contain whey, cheese, or casein. Pretzels, popcorn and saltines are often okay. Potato and corn chips are mostly all free of dairy and soy also. Be careful to avoid "flavored" varieties chips, popcorn or pretzels, many of the flavorings contain cheese, or whey as an emulsifier.

Cookies—it is hard to find a commercial brand or bakery cookie that is acceptable on this diet, though there are a few. I found the best alternative was to make my own. Like snack crackers, many cookies contain milk products such as whey, butter fat, casein, and nonfat dry milk.

Chocolate—there are a few brands of semi-sweet chocolate are acceptable, they are: **Enjoy** semi-sweet chocolate chips, **Sunspire, Chocolate Dream** chocolate bars and chips, Whole Food's 365 brand dark chocolate chunks, **Newmann's Own** semi-sweet chocolate bars, and **Cloud Nine** semi-sweet chocolate and chocolate chips. Though many other commercial brands of dark or semi-sweet chocolate do not include milk, or dairy in their ingredients, they are processed on lines, or in factories that also process milk products, so you cannot be completely sure that they are clean. Don't be fooled by ingredient names such as cocoa butter: it contains no butter, rather it refers to the "meat' of the cocoa bean. Soy lecithin is also acceptable; it is a fat, used primarily as an emulsifier, not a protein.

Candy—Most chewy, gummy fruit candies are okay, as are many hard candies, except those that contain caramel or chocolate. Caramel or other flavorings may contain milk products.

Candy Bars—could not find any acceptable commercial brands.

Cakes—you will not be able to eat desserts out at a restaurant or bakery, but you can make cakes and brownies at home that are okay to eat. If you do not have time for the scratch cake recipes found in the cookbook section, many of **Duncan Hines** brand cake and brownie mixes are without milk or soy protein. If you write, or call Duncan Hines, they will send you a listing of all their mixes that are dairy/soy protein free. Some of their ready-made frostings are also dairy-free.

Other—plain rice krispy bars are okay (including those manufactured by Kellogg's). Marshmallows and marshmallow cremes are generally okay.

Ice cream and other **frozen desserts**—so many great varieties out now. My favorites are the coconut milk ice creams, though some of the almond milk frozen treats are quite delicious too. Some favorites are **So Delicious, Larry** and **Luna's Coconut Bliss, Almond Dream** and **Rice Dream** ice cream's and frozen treats. Also chocolate dipped bananas.

Breakfast

Cereals—many of the popular commercial cereals are okay, but read labels carefully. Watch out for single serving packaged hot-cereal varieties, many contain milk products.

Breakfast Bars—some of **Kellogg's** PopTart® flavors are okay, but nearly all other brand contain milk products in the breading base. Larabar, and many other natural bars are okay as well

Pancakes/Waffles—whether a packaged mix or frozen varieties most all contain milk and soy products. Much safer to make your own.

Bagels—bagels from many franchise bakeries such as Einstein's or Bruegger's make several varieties of bagels without milk and\or soy. Watch for the added ingredients in bagels such as "jalapeno cheddar."

Muffins, **sweetrolls** and **doughnuts**—bad news here: most all commercial brands (including Krispy Kreme) contain nonfat dry milk and possibly other milk and\or soy ingredients. Making your own is always the best choice.

Other Carbohydrates:

Pasta—most all varieties fresh or dried pasta are okay to use. Boxed pasta mixes with sauces will generally contain milk and\or soy products.

Rice—like pasta, dry rice, steamed or cooked in water is fine. Many boxed mixes, however, will contain milk and\or soy. Read all labels carefully.

Breads—commercially baked breads and dough products can be tricky. The majority of the breads on the market will contain nonfat dry milk, whey, milk solids, and or soy flour, and possibly some other milk\soy products. Look for French or Italian breads, go to a bakery and check out their selection. Many grocery chains will bake fresh French or Italian breads that do not contain milk or soy. Go to a bread bakery, such as Great Harvest, many of their breads are suitable as well. Look for kosher or parve symbols on bread wrappers such as Rotella which makes many varieties of bread and rolls that are without milk and soy.

*Watch out for breading. Nearly all breading for fried chicken, nuggets, fried or baked fish and more contain milk and\or soy. Also, bread crumbs that may be used as filler in meatballs, meatloaf and burgers often contain nonfat dry milk, whey, and even some soy proteins.

Other Grains: Farro, Quinoa, Kamut and Millet are all ancient grains that are getting much easier to find. Use them for salads, sides, breakfasts, you can substitute them for oats or bulgar wheat in most any recipe.

Beverages

Juices are okay. Look for the juices that contain added calcium for an extra boost—you will need to take a calcium supplement while on this diet. Check with your physician or Dietician, but most recommend 1200mg Calcium per day while pregnant or breastfeeding. Pure vegetable juices are excellent as well. Go to your local juice bar for a treat, just watch for added yogurt, milk, or soy.

Hot drinks such as coffee, tea and chai are okay as long as there is no added milk. You can use the packaged Chai (concentrate) and add your own coconut, almond or rice milk. Do be careful of instant flavored coffees, lattes, cappuccino and tea, many contain milk products. Most instant hot cocoa varieties contain milk products as well.

Soups—watch out for soy protein in most commercial brand soups. Swanson's Natural Goodness brand chicken broth is the only brand I found that did not contain soy protein. Pacific Natural Foods has many soups, broths, side dishes and beverages, including hemp, almond, hazelnut, rice and oat milks. The Pacific foods website also offers a food allergy filter where you can chose your allergies or intolerances and it shows you the foods that fit your diet.

Check labels carefully.

Fruits and Vegetables

Fruits—fresh fruits are always great to eat and good for you too! Dried fruits are also an excellent source of vitamins and fiber, but are also high in sugar. Keep some frozen fruits on hand for "milk" shakes. Slice and freeze ripe bananas and use in shakes, or to dip in chocolate.

Vegetables—fresh vegetables, like fruits, are very good for you. Keep cut up carrots and other vegetables handy for snacking. Watch out for sauces on frozen vegetables. The labeling will give you clues, like "buttery" or "light" sauce; then, as always, read the label carefully.

Protein

Meats/Fish—all fresh and frozen plain meats and fish are okay. Watch out for breaded meats and fish, the breading will usually contain milk and\or soy. There is often added soy protein in processed packaged meats, such as premade hamburgers, and meatballs and in some varieties of reduced fat hot dogs, and other meats. There is also soy protein in most hamburger substitutes, such as GardenBurgers or Boca Burgers.

Beans—beans area an excellent source of protein and are used throughout this cookbook in a variety of recipes. As with many foods that are gaseous, beans may cause your baby some distress. If you think they are a source of upset to your baby, simply eliminate them for a period to see if the fussiness, gassiness subsides.

*If you are vegetarian, or vegan, please consult a dietician to help with planning your diet so you get enough protein and calcium I prefer not to eat a large amount of meat in my diet, however, I found that during pregnancy I had to add more lean meat for the protein I needed.

A word about **kosher/parve** symbols: items that are labeled parve or parve do not contain any animal products, so, there will be no milk products in these items. A certified Kosher symbol (the symbol is an encircled "K") means that the product was not made on machinery or with cooking utensils that products containing animal products were made on or with. You will see the both the kosher and parve symbol on Fleischmann's unsalted margarine and on many packages of Rotella bread. I used these symbols to help me pick out dairy-free foods, but also checked the labels as well.

MANUFACTURER\PRODUCT LISTINGS

http://www.almondie.com/making-almond-milk.aspx—almond milk concentrate, almond milk, nut butters, oils

http://www.califiafarms.com—almond milk and almond/coconut blends, Almond milk espresso, latte and mocha beverage—really good stuff!

http://www.earthbalancenatural.com/product/soy-free-buttery-spread/—great products, I still use this margarine long because it is really good. Culinary spreads, dressings, nut butters, baking sticks, shortening, tub margarine and snacks.

http://www.veganeasy.org/Vegan-Pantry—great place to get information on products, some have soy, but many dairy and soy free listings. Find shelf stable Hemp, Oat, Aussie Dream Rice Milk.

http://www.goveggiefoods.com—dairy, soy free cheeses, cream cheese, parmesan like grated topping.

http://almondbreeze.com—Blue Diamond Almond beverages, some shelf stable, lattes, almond coconut blends.

http://silk.com/products—almond milk, light almond milk, coconut milk and recipes on this website.

http://us.daiyafoods.com/—dairy, soy free cheeses, cream cheeses.

www.sodeliciousdairyfree.com—coconut and almond milk beverages, creamers, yogurts and coconut milk ice cream—all very good.

http://www.spectrumorganics.com—oils, mayonnaises, cooking spray, all organic, recipes.

http://www.pacificfoods.com—broths, soups, meals, sides, sauces, purees, beverages. This site has a special diet filter, you filter out then foods, or substances you can't eat, and it tells you which products you can eat.

www.rightfoods.com—McDougall's foods, dairy free, free of most soy—avoid the asian bowls as some have soy in the sauce. Oatmeal bowls, soups, quinoa, most are ready to go, just add hot water.

www.duncanhines.com—baking mixes, most are dairy and soy free, recipes and baking ideas. Ingredients are accessible once you click on the mix you want.

http://coconutbliss.com/—amazing flavors of coconut milk ice cream and frozen treats. Definitely the top of the line.

http://www.cherrybrookkitchen.com/—baking mixes for cakes, muffins, pancakes, frostings, allergy friendly products

http://www.ahlaska.com/—great dairy and soy free chocolate syrup, however the baking cocoa is no longer completely dairy or soy free, the allergen statement now says it is now processed on a line that also processes milk and soy.

http://www.premiumchocolatiers.com—milk chocolate style bars and treats, careful the white chocolate contains soy, but the "milk" and dark chocolate bars so not. No nuts either.

http://followyourheart.com/products—dairy and soy free vegannaise, dressings, cheeses.

http://www.enjoylifefoods.com—dairy, soy and gluten free chocolate ships for baking, snacks, cookies.

http://us.daiyafoods.com—dairy, soy free cheeses, slices and wedge cheese, cream cheese and pizzas.

www.fantasticfoods.com—convenient cereals, meals and soups in a microwaveable cup. Other products include pasta and rice mixes. Not all are milk\soy protein free, so read labels carefully.

www.namastefoods.com/products—dairy, soy and gluten free foods.

www.imaginefoods.com—creamy soups and broths. These are excellent products.

www.tastethedream.com/products-rice, almond, coconut and even sunflower milk, frozen treats also.

www.nilespice.com—soup and couscous bowls, just add hot water.

www.neareast.com—many mixes are milk\soy protein free and are excellent: falafel mix, rice and couscous mixes.

http://www.tropicaltraditions.com—dairy free cocoa, and other products such as coconut oil, skin care and supplements.

www.newmansownorganics.com—semi-sweet chocolate bars in plain, sweet orange and espresso. There are many other great products and recipes too.

OTHER RESOURCES AND SUPPORT SITES

www.breastfeedingboutique.com—Methodist Lactation Specialists, thanks you for all the support you have given MSPI Guide. Great support and all the equipment and supplies you need for success.

http://bosombuddiesomaha.com—big supporter of MSPI Guide—thank you Deb. Private consultation for breastfeeding.

www.alegentcreighton.com/lactation-support—lactation specialists.

www.milkworks.org—Lincoln, Nebraska lactation specialists.

http://www.omahabutterfly.com/ibclcbreastfeedingsupport.htm—Omaha resources and support.

http://mommywisdomblog.blogspot.com—Omaha MSPI blog—great site.

www.mspimama.com—this is a really good site, my compliments. Great information and support for MSPI moms.

http://www.lalecheleague.org/nb.html—breastfeeding support

http://www.bigcitybelly.com/2011/10/my-favorite-dairy-and-soy-free-foods/—great blog; really good information and comments from readers.

http://www.milkfreekids.com/p/dairy-free-foods.html—great resources, information and support.

http://www.thiswifebakes.com/2011/03/dairy-free-soy-free-cake-and-frosting.html—great blog and recipes.

http://www.kiwimagonline.com/?recipe=dairy-free-vanilla-frosting—this is a good website for natural and organic parenting.

http://dairyfreecooking.about.com/od/techniquessubstitutions/tp/soysubstitutes.htm—soy-free dairy substitutes and recipes.

http://www.twopeasandtheirpod.com/vegan-coconut-raspberry-ice-cream/—a great blog for recipes; vegan websites are terrific for this diet, just watch for the soy.

http://chocolatecoveredkatie.com—a great website for special diets and natural foods.

http://kellymom.com—breastfeeding, parenting and support

www.skyisland.com/ online resources—Information on food allergies and intolerances, online cookbook and a substitutions page.

www.foodallergy.org—information on food allergies, cookbooks and nutrition.

http://www.cdc.gov/breastfeeding/resources/guide.htm

www.wholehealthmd.com—general information on health, diet and natural healing. Includes a reference library, shopping and recipes.

www.mothers.org—information on mothering, products, foods and much more.

www.simplysogood.com—blog on cooking/baking. I love this blog.

www.montanarob.homestead.com—home of the "No Moo" cookbook and other information on milk allergies and intolerance.

www.geocites.com/hotspring/4620/.—no nonsense information on soy allergies.

http://www.wholefoodlifestyles.com—this is a really good blog dedicated to whole foods recipes, dairy, soy and gluten free.

SPECIAL CIRCUMSTANCES

EatingOut . . .

There are a few places you can go and not have to worry, Whole Foods, Chipotle, Qdoba, (just avoid the cheese and sour cream), and natural foods eateries.

My best advice on eating out is to call ahead, unless you know the menu. I would first explain my special circumstances and then ask if there were items on their menu that might be milk/soy protein free. To my surprise in most every restaurant I called their was someone who would take the time to go through the menu with me and even read ingredients off labels for me, in fact I often talked directly to the chef.

One of my oldest son's favorite restaurants was a local burger restaurant, they took the time to tell me about the meat (no fillers in the hamburger), and read through the label on the hamburger buns which let me know that I could eat the burgers, but not the buns. Which brings me to another piece of advice . . .

Bring items with you that you know are milk/soy protein free. I always brought my own hamburger buns to the fore-mentioned restaurant, and if I was going to have salad, I brought my own salad dressing. To my surprise, no one ever said a word about it. Items that I frequently brought out with me were: margarine, buns, bread, salad dressings and maybe a cookie, or a piece of chocolate if I knew everyone else would be having dessert. That way, I never had to feel left out.

In choosing menu items, I always figured that grilled meat was pretty safe, as long as they didn't baste it in butter or marinade containing soy sauce. Most salads were okay also, as long as they were made without cheese, croutons, and served with the dressing on the side. I would always let my waiter know what my needs were as well, that way they could help guide me in my choices.

Eateries like Chipotle will even change their gloves for you if they could have previously handled cheese.

If you are really lucky, your town has a kosher deli! What a goldmine! There you can be assured that no bread will contain milk products, because kosher law forbids the mixing of milk products with meat. And you can, for the same reason, trust the soups. Just make sure bread and soups do not contain any soy flour or soy protein. Health food, or "natural food" restaurants are also terrific; they are used to catering to special needs.

When invited out for dinner . . . again, call ahead. I would always call the host or hostess a few days before the date, explain my special circumstances, and ask about the menu. I never wanted anyone to feel like they had to change the menu for me, but that it would help me to know what is planned in advance so I could bring anything I needed to supplement my meal. Then, I would always ask to bring something, dessert was my usual offering, that way I knew I could at least indulge in dessert with everyone else!

Outdoor potluck dinners on the grill were particularly easy, you could bring your own meat, margarine for a baked potato, salad dressing and dessert. One time that we were invited out, the hostess was planning lasagna, salad, and vegetables. I brought a grilled chicken breast, and my own dressing and had it over salad, and of course, I offered to bring some dessert so I could partake as well.

Fast food . . . Always call the 1-800 numbers each of the fast food, or chain restaurants, (or for that matter food manufacturers) make available. You will speak with someone who usually has nutritional information at their fingertips. For instance, I called Taco Bell's 1-800 # and they were able to go through the ingredients on their flour tortillas, their guacamole, and their refried beans which are all milk\soy protein free. So, I could have a bean burrito, minus the cheese (which I usually replaced with lettuce and tomato, or guacamole), and a 7-layer burrito, minus the cheese and sour cream. This gave me a fast food alternative that I really liked. Choose the fast food restaurant that you enjoy most and call them, explore the options that are available to you.

You do become the "food police" when on this diet, knowing that it you mess up, you and your child will pay for it. So you will become very suspicious, but don't feel bad about asking questions, most people are more than willing to help you wade your way through a pile of ingredients.

APPETIZERS

Black Bean Rollups

4-10 inch flour tortillas
1-15 ounce can black beans, drained
1/4 cup lime juice
2 green onions chopped
1/8 cup cilantro, minced
1/2 cup yellow pepper, chopped
1/4 cup green olives, chopped
1/2 teaspoon garlic salt

Puree beans in a food processor or blender. Stir in rice milk, onion, cilantro and garlic salt. Spread bean mixture evenly over 4 tortillas. Top with even amounts yellow pepper and green olives. Roll tortilla up tightly and wrap. Chill in refrigerator 1-2 hours. Cut into 3/4 inch slices to serve. Serve with salsa, and\or guacamole (next recipe).

Guacamole

3 ripe avocados, peeled and mashed
1 teaspoon onion powder
1 teaspoon garlic salt
1 cup roma tomatoes, diced
1 tablespoon lime juice

Mix seasoning, tomatoes and lime juice into avocado and stir well. Refrigerate before serving. Serve with tortilla chips, or crackers. Great with burrito and other mexican fare.

Chile Lime Hummus

2 15-ounce cans garbanzo beans, drained
1/3 cup tahini (sesame seed paste)
1/3 cup lime juice
1-2 Tablespoons olive oil
2 tablespoons cider vinegar
1 tablespoon minced garlic
1/2 teaspoon chile powder
1 teaspoon seasoning salt
1/4 teaspoon red pepper flakes, or more if you wish

Combine all ingredients in food processor and blend until smooth. Use as a spread on bread, pita, crackers, or tortillas.

Stuffed Mushrooms

20-24 mushrooms, washed, stems removed, reserved and chopped
2 tablespoons olive oil
1 tablespoon Earth Balance margarine
1 teaspoon garlic, minced
2/3 cup red bell pepper, diced
2 green onions, chopped
1 & 1/2 tablespoons parsley, minced
1/2 cup bread crumbs
1/2 teaspoon chile powder
1 & 1/2 teaspoons salt
all-vegetable cooking spray

In a medium skillet, combine olive oil and garlic. Heat over medium heat until garlic is light golden brown. Sauté together chopped mushroom stems, bell pepper, onion until slightly tender, 2 to 3 minutes. Add parsley and bread crumbs and sauté 1 to 2 more minutes. Remove from heat, add chile powder and salt. Set aside and cool.

Spray a large baking dish with cooking spray. Spoon stuffing into the mushroom caps, distribute evenly. Place stuffed mushroom caps in baking dish. At this point, mushroom caps may be covered and refrigerated for several hours. When ready to serve, preheat oven to 400 degrees. Place baking dish in upper third of oven and bake 10 to 15 minutes until bubbly and tender.

Eggplant and Garlic Spread

1 large eggplant
4 garlic cloves, peeled
2 tablespoons olive oil
juice of 1/4th a lemon
1 teaspoon oregano flakes
1/2 teaspoon cumin powder
1 teaspoon salt
all-vegetable cooking spray

Preheat oven to 450 degrees. Cut eggplant in half and place in baking dish sprayed with cooking spray, cut side down. Slip 2 garlic cloves under each eggplant halve, and bake for 1 hour, or until tender. Cool.

Scrape pulp from eggplant halves, drain in colander, until excess moisture is gone. Place eggplant pulp, garlic, oil, lemon juice, oregano and seasoning in food processor. Process until smooth. May use more salt and pepper to taste. Use as a spread with crackers, vegetables, bread or pita.

Pesto Pizza

1 dough recipe (page 43)
1 pesto recipe (page 51)
1 package sun-dried tomatoes

Roll, or press out dough into a large round. Poke holes in top of dough with a fork. Spread pesto gently over top of dough, then add sun-dried tomatoes evenly over surface. Can add Daiya Mozzarella shreds if desired.

Bake at 400 degrees for 10 to 15 minutes, until dough is puffed and golden brown. Keep an eye on this while baking so that sun-dried tomatoes do not burn.

Roasted Tomato Spread

2 containers grape tomatoes, rinse and cut in half
2 handfuls basil leaves, shredded
2 teaspoons minced garlic
3-4 teaspoons olive oil

Preheat oven to 300 degrees. Mix all ingredients together in a large bowl (I use my hands). Spread on a baking sheet lined with non-stick foil. Roast for 1 and 1/2 to 2 hours. Check at half hour intervals and stir. The tomatoes may char a bit, and that is fine, it gives the pesto great flavor. Cool, scrape into a small bowl and season with salt—careful not too much, the roasting process does give the tomatoes a salty taste.

I especially love making this spread with fresh summer tomatoes—it is divine.

But it is also good made with store bought grape tomatoes. Spread it on french bread, or pita chips, great as a sandwich spread. In the summer I make this frequently and freeze small batches; it is also good as a pasta sauce.

BEVERAGES

These recipes may be made with your choice of alternative "milk," sweetened or not, depending on your preference.

Banana Shake

8 ounces enriched "milk," chilled
1 banana, sliced (may be fresh or frozen)
1/4 cup crushed ice

Put all ingredients into blender and blend until smooth. Serve immediately. (this shake is especially good with the dark chocolate almond milk)

Healthy Breakfast Shake

8 ounces enriched "milk," chilled (good with half "milk" and Orange Juice)
1 banana, sliced
1/2 teaspoon vanilla, or almond extract
1 tablespoon wheat germ
1/4 teaspoon cinnamon

Put all ingredients into blender and blend until smooth. Serve immediately.

Key Lime Smoothie

Juice of one lime
1 scoop egg white protein powder
1/2 teaspoon vanilla
1/2 grated lime zest
1 teaspoon coconut, flaked, unsweetened
1 cup almond or coconut milk (flavored varieties are good here too) sweetener to taste

Blend all ingredients together with 1/2 cup crushed ice.

Tropical Fruit Shake

1 cup vanilla frozen dessert (coconut is my favorite)
1/3 cup pineapple juice
1/4 cup orange juice
1 ripe banana, sliced
Put all ingredients into blender and blend until smooth. Serve immediately.

Berry Smoothie

1/2 cup frozen strawberries
1/4 cup frozen blueberries
1/4 cup frozen raspberries
1 cup enriched "milk," chilled

Place all ingredients into blender and puree until smooth. Sweeten to taste with Agave syrup. Serve immediately.

Banana-Strawberry Shake

1/2 cup frozen strawberries
1 ripe banana, sliced
1 cup enriched rice milk, chilled

Place all ingredients into blender and blend until smooth. Sweeten to taste. Serve immediately.

Chocolate Raspberry Shake

1/2 cup frozen raspberries
1 cup enriched chocolate "milk," chilled
1/2 teaspoon vanilla extract
1 tablespoon Ah!laska dairy free chocolate syrup

Place all ingredients into blender and blend until smooth. Sweeten to taste. Serve immediately.

Peach-Berry Shake

1/2 cup frozen peaches
1/2 cup frozen raspberries
1 cup enriched vanilla "milk," or frozen dessert

Place all ingredients into blender and blend until smooth. Sweeten to taste. Serve immediately.

Chocolate PB Banana shake

8 ounces Dark Chocolate Almond milk
2 tablespoons PB2, peanut butter powder
1 banana, frozen in slices
Sweetener to taste
Blend all until smooth and creamy. Yum.

Orange Banana Fiber Shake

1 ripe banana, frozen and sliced
4 orange flavored prunes, chopped
1/2 cup orange juice
1 cup enriched "milk," chilled

Place all ingredients into blender and blend until smooth. Serve immediately.

**Tips for shakes: Take over-ripe bananas and slice, wrap in plastic and freeze. Using frozen bananas helps thicken up the shake. If bananas are fresh, may use 1/4 cup crushed ice to thicken. Add 1 tablespoon bran or wheat germ or Beneful to boost the fiber in your shake. Some are not terribly sweet, so you may want to add Agave syrup or your choice sweetener to desired sweetness.

Use your choice of "milk" or flavored syrups to create your favorite smoothie.

Hot Beverages

Chai

1 cup Chai concentrate
1 cup enriched "milk"

Heat together in a microwave-safe mug, about 2 to 3 minutes. Stir and serve.

Vanilla Chai

1 cup Chai concentrate
1 cup, or more, enriched vanilla "milk"

Heat together in a microwave-safe mug, about 2 to 3 minutes. Stir and serve.

Chocolate Chai

1 cup chai concentrate
1 cup enriched dark chocolate "milk"
1 tablespoon Ah!laska chocolate dairy free syrup

Heat together in a microwave-safe mug, about 2 to 3 minutes. Add mini marshmallows, stir and serve.

Hot Cocoa

1/2 cup Ah!laska chocolate dairy free syrup
1/2 cup granulated sugar
4 cups enriched "milk"

Stir ingredients together in a medium saucepan over medium heat. Heat thoroughly while stirring, but do not allow to boil. Makes 4-1 cup servings or 2 larger servings. Marshmallows are optional!

Cafe Latté

1/2 cup strong coffee or espresso
1 cup enriched "milk"
1-2 ounces flavored coffee syrup (vanilla, almond, irish creme, etc.)

Heat all coffee and "milk" together in a microwave-safe mug, about 2 to 3 minutes. Stir in syrup and serve.

I love having a coconut milk latté—delicious!

BREADS, BREAKFASTS AND BRUNCH

Pumpkin Oatmeal

1 and 1/2 cups water (or all milk of choice, for a creamier oatmeal)
1 cup coconut or almond milk
1 cup Coach's Oats (my favorite brand)
pinch of salt
1 cup pumpkin puree
1/2 teaspoon pumpkin pie spice

Combine liquid and Oats in a medium saucepan and bring to a boil, reduce heat, and simmer for about 5 minutes. Stir in pumpkin, pie spice and salt and cook until heated through. Serves 4, 1/2 cup servings.

Enjoy with Brown Sugar, extra coconut or almond milk or margarine. A little bit of orange juice or zest will brighten up the pumpkin flavor.

Breakfast Quinoa

1 cup Quinoa
2 cups water
pinch salt
1/2 cup chopped walnuts
1 diced apple, granny smith is good
1/2 teaspoon cinnamon
1/2 teaspoon vanilla extract
Almond or coconut milk
Brown sugar

Bring small saucepan with water to a boil, add salt and quinoa, cook for about 15 minutes until water is absorbed. Stir in walnuts, apple, cinnamon, vanilla and a splash of coconut or almond milk, just so you are able to stir well. Heat thoroughly, pass the brown sugar and dig in. Serves 2-4, depending on the helping.

Tamara Field

Pumpkin Pancakes

2 cups flour
1 and 1/2 tablespoons baking powder
2 tablespoons brown sugar
2 eggs, or egg substitute
1 cup pumpkin puree
2 teaspoons vanilla
2 cups coconut milk
1 teaspoon pumpkin pie spice
1 teaspoon cinnamon

Combine dry ingredients in large bowl, in another bowl whisk brown sugar, eggs, vanilla, spices and milk. Pour wet mixture over dry, slowly stirring in. You may need to add a bit more milk if batter seems to thick.

Heat griddle and make pancakes, whatever size or shape you'd like. Serve these with warm maple syrup.

Pumpkin Scones

2 cups flour
1/2 cup brown sugar
1 tablespoon baking powder
1/2 teaspoon salt
1 teaspoon pumpkin pie spice
6 tablespoons margarine
1 egg
1/2 cup pureed pumpkin*
3 tablespoons coconut milk
Preheat oven to 350 degrees.

This recipe is easiest to make in a food processor. just add all the dry ingredients and pulse to combine. Then add margarine and pulse until crumbly and coarse. In a small bowl whisk together the pumpkin, egg and coconut milk and pour into dry mix, pulsing to combine.

Take dough out and knead a few times on a floured surface until dough is soft and together. flatten dough into a pie pan coated with cooking spray. Score the top of the dough in 6 pieces.

Bake for 12-15 minutes until just turning golden. Remove from oven and cool, top with coconut cream glaze.

*instead of pumpkin, you could use 2 overripe bananas mashed, 1 cup of diced apple or pear, or 1 cup finely grated zucchini. Use your imagination and adjust the spices accordingly. Add-ins: I like the pumpkin scones with mini semisweet chocolate chips, but you could add in nuts, coconut, or citrus zest.

Coconut Cream Glaze

1 cup powdered sugar
2-3 teaspoons coconut creamer, or coconut milk
Whisk together until smooth and drizzle over scones.

Zucchini-Potato Frittata

8 eggs
2 tablespoons enriched "milk"
2 tablespoons margarine
1 medium zucchini, diced
1/2 red bell pepper
1 medium red potato, diced (small pieces)
1 tablespoon toasted dried minced onion
1/4 cup flaked nutritional yeast, or Daiya cheddar shreds
1/2 teaspoon garlic salt
all-vegetable cooking spray

In a medium bowl, beat eggs with milk and minced onion, and seasoning. Set aside. Heat a 10-inch non-stick cast iron (or ovenproof) skillet to medium high heat. Add margarine and melt. Sauté potato until lightly browned, then place lid on and steam. Add zucchini and bell pepper and sauté for about five minutes Preheat oven to broil. Reduce heat on stove to medium and add egg mixture. As eggs begin to cook, lift the edges with a spatula so the uncooked eggs will flow underneath and cook.

Repeat until the egg mixture is cooked. Remove from stove top and place in the oven broil 3 to 4 minutes until top is golden brown. Remove, cool and serve.

Southwest Strata

1 cup enriched "milk"
4 eggs
1 green onion, chopped
2 tablespoons diced green chiles
2 cups white bread, torn into bite-sized pieces
1 small can sliced or minced black olives
1/4-1/3 cup nutritional yeast flakes or Daiya Cheddar shreds
All-vegetable cooking spray

Preheat oven to 400 degrees. Coat a 10-inch quiche or pie plate With cooking spray. Whisk together milk and eggs. Stir in green onion and green chiles. Add bread and stir until well blended. Transfer mixture into prepared baking dish. Let egg mixture set so bread can soak up moisture, about 10 minutes.

Bake, uncovered, until lightly browned, and puffed up, about 25 to 30 minutes. Serve with salsa and avocado.

Overnight French Toast

1 cup packed brown sugar
1 stick margarine
1 tablespoon light corn syrup
12 slices white bread, crusts removed (about 12 oz. bread)
1 & 1/2 cups enriched vanilla almond or coconut milk
6 large eggs (egg substitute may be used)
1/4 teaspoon salt
2 teaspoons cinnamon
all-vegetable cooking spray

Combine brown sugar, margarine and corn syrup in small saucepan. Bring to a boil over medium heat while stirring constantly. Allow mixture to boil 5 minutes still slightly thickened. Pour mixture into a 13 x 9 inch pan, coated with cooking spray, and spread until mixture covers the bottom of the pan.

Arrange bread slices over the brown sugar mixture in pan, double layering bread.

Whisk eggs, rice milk, cinnamon and salt. Pour over bread. Cover and refrigerate overnight. Bake at 350 degrees until light golden brown and bread is puffed. Let cool 10 minutes, then serve warm. Invert servings onto dessert plates so the caramel sauce runs over the bread. Great with Cranberry Salsa.

**Variations: add 1 /2 cup chopped pecans, raisins, or dried cranberries to the caramel layer before adding, bread.

Cranberry Salsa

1 can crushed pineapple, drained
2 cans mandarin oranges, drained
1 can whole cranberry sauce
1/2 cup chopped walnuts
Mix fruit and nuts together. Chill before serving

Pancakes

1 cup all-purpose flour
1/2 cup oats
1 teaspoon baking soda
1/4 teaspoon salt
1 & 1/4 cups "milk"
2 tablespoons margarine, melted
1 egg

Combine dry ingredients in a medium mixing bowl. In a small bowl, whisk together milk, margarine, and egg. Add to flour mixture and stir until smooth. Heat a non-stick griddle over medium high heat. Spoon batter onto griddle. Turn when tops of pancakes are all bubbly.

Makes 10 to 12 pancakes. Serve with margarine and syrup.

**Variations: blueberries, mini chocolate chips, or 1 teaspoon cinnamon.

Cinnamon French Toast

2 eggs
3/4 cup enriched vanilla "milk"
1 teaspoon cinnamon
1/4 teaspoon nutmeg
8 slices thick french bread
confectioners sugar

Whisk together eggs, rice milk, and spices. Heat a non-stick skillet over medium high heat. Dip bread slices in egg mixture then place in skillet. Cook until golden brown on each side, turning once. Arrange on plate, dust with confectioners powder.

**Great served with sliced bananas, or peanut butter and maple syrup.

Pumpkin Bread

2 cups flour
2 teaspoons baking soda
1/2 teaspoon salt
1/2 cup vanilla almond or coconut milk
1 15 ounce can pumpkin puree
2 teaspoons vanilla extract
3/4 cup brown sugar
1/2 cup canola oil
1 egg (can be made with just egg white, or egg replacer if desired).
2 teaspoons pumpkin pie spice

Additions: mini chocolate chips, dried cherries or cranberries, walnuts.

Preheat oven to 350 degrees. Spray 2 loaf pans with cooking spray (I like Trader Joe's coconut oil spray).

Mix pumpkin, sugar, egg, oil, and vanilla, stirring until smooth. Mix dry ingredients together, and add to pumpkin mixture alternating with milk.

Stir in any additions.

Pour into prepared pans, bake 40-45 minutes until a toothpick comes clean in the center of the pan, and bread looks set. Turn off heat and leave the loaves to cool in the oven.

Cranberry Orange Crusty Bread

4 cups all-purpose flour
1/2 teaspoon kosher salt
1 teaspoon dry yeast
2 cups warm water
2 tablespoons honey
juice and zest of one medium orange
dried cranberries, chopped
walnuts, chopped *optional

Place flour and salt in a large mixing bowl. In a smaller bowl whisk yeast into warm water and add honey, let proof 5-10 minutes until bubbly. Add orange juice, zest, cranberries and *walnuts to flour mixture and stir, then add water/yeast to flour while stirring with a wooden spoon. Once dough is well-blended, cover with a towel and let rise in a warm place.

You can leave the dough like this 2-3 hrs or all day. Once dough is doubled, heavily dust a clean surface with flour. Pour dough out on the floured surface. With floured hands gently knead more flour into the dough, just until it is smooth and moldable; dough will still be pretty soft. Roughly shape into 2 rounds, and cover for 1-2 hours.

I bake this bread, and all my bread using the technique I learned on the "simplysogood" blog. It makes a delicious crusty bread that turns out perfect every time.

So while the dough is in it's final rise, preheat the oven to 450 degrees. Once oven is at 450, place a clay pot with lid, or a cast iron dutch oven in the oven to heat, heat the clay/dutch oven for 30 minutes. Carefully take the lid off the pot and put the dough gently in the bottom. You do not have to arrange it, it will form a nice round or rectangular loaf as it bakes. Place the lid back on the pot/dutch oven and bake for 35-40 minutes until the bread is golden brown.

Carefully take the pot out of the oven, wait about 10 minutes then remove the loaf—it will come right out.

This bread is fantastic! Thank you to www.simplysogood.com for the guidance.

SALADS

Farro with Apricots, Pistachios and Herbs

Farro is an ancient grain that is making a comeback. It is intensely nutty and chewy, you could also substitute brown rice, kamut, wheat berries, or bulgar wheat.

2 cups Farro
1/2 cup minced yellow onion
2 teaspoons minced garlic
3 tablespoons olive oil
1/2 cup diced dried apricots
1/2 cup parsley minced
1/2 cup cilantro minced
1/2 cup pistachios, chopped
juice of one lemon

Bring 4 cups water to a boil and add the farro, reduce heat and place lid on pot to simmer. Heat the olive oil in a skillet and sauté the onion and garlic until soft. Once farro is tender, about 30 minutes, drain and add the onion, garlic mixture to the grain. Stir in the herbs, pistachios, apricots and lemon, salt and pepper to taste.

Black Bean and Rice Salad

2 & 1/2 cups chicken broth
1 & 1/4 cups white rice (long grain)
1 15-ounce can black beans, rinsed and drained
1 pound plum tomatoes, seeded and chopped (about 6)
1/2 cup green bell pepper, chopped
1/2 cup yellow bell pepper, chopped
1 cup chopped onion (vidalia, or sweet variety)
1/4 cup cider vinegar
2 tablespoons olive oil
juice of 1 lime
1 tablespoon chopped garlic
1 tablespoon chopped cilantro

Bring chicken broth to boil in a large saucepan; add rice, cover pan and simmer over reduced heat until tender (about 20 minutes). Transfer to a large bowl and cool to room temperature.

Add black beans, tomato, peppers and onion to rice and mix well. In a separate small bowl whisk remainder of the ingredients together. Pour dressing over salad and toss. Add salt and pepper to taste. Serve at room temperature.

White Bean Salad

2 16-ounce cans great northern beans, rinsed and drained
1 & 1/2 cups plum tomatoes, chopped
1/2 cup sweet onion, chopped
2 tablespoons olive oil
1 clove garlic, chopped
1/4 cup parsley, chopped
juice of 1/2 lemon
1/4 cup white vinegar

Heat 1 tablespoon olive oil over medium high heat and sauté garlic till just browned. Remove from heat. Add garlic to remaining tablespoon olive oil, whisk in parsley, lemon juice and vinegar until blended.

In a large bowl, combine beans, tomato and onion. Pour dressing over top and toss. Chill and then serve.

Israeli Couscous Salad

1 box or package Israeli couscous (larger than most couscous, like fish eggs)
grape or Roma tomatoes diced
1 cucumber diced (preferably one without seeds)
1 yellow or orange bell pepper diced
2 green onions, diced
1 cup minced parsley
1/2 cup sliced Kalmata olives
2 tablespoons olive oil
Juice of one lemon

Cook couscous according to package, drain. Mix all vegetables, olives and parsley, olive oil and lemon thoroughly with couscous, serve.

Curried Couscous Salad

1 package couscous, I like the Israeli type
2 scallions, chopped
1/2 dried cranberries
1/2 cup chopped pecans
1/4 cup minced parsley
chicken broth

Cook couscous according to package substituting chicken broth for water. Drain and fluff couscous, add in other ingredients and toss, chill.

Sautéed Cajun Salad

8 cup mixed spring greens
Italian salad dressing
juice of 1 lemon
2 tablespoon olive oil
1 pound (16 ounces) cooked medium shrimp
1 small package turkey pepperoni
1 cup onion, coarsely chopped
1 red bell pepper, coarsely chopped
2 garlic cloves, chopped
1 cup canned black beans, rinsed and drained
1-2 tablespoons cajun seasoning, to taste
2 granny smith apples, sliced in wedges (about 8 per apple), not peeled

Divide spring greens evenly among serving plates.

Heat oil in a large skillet over medium heat. Add onion, red pepper and garlic and sauté 2-3 minutes. Without reducing heat, add shrimp and pepperoni and cook an additional 5 minutes while stirring constantly (stir fry style). Reduce heat to medium and add black beans and cajun spice, stirring well and frequently. Add apples and cook an other 1-2 minutes until heated.

Drizzle Italian salad dressing over spring greens and then divide sautéed mixture evenly and spoon over prepared salad. Serve while still warm. Serves 4.

Tabbouleh

3 cups fresh parsley, minced
1/3 cup fresh mint leaves, minced
2 cups cucumber, chopped
2 cups roma tomatoes, chopped
1/2 cup green onion, chopped
1 4-ounce can chopped black olives
1 & 1/2 cups bulgar or cracked wheat, uncooked
2 tablespoons olive oil
juice of 1 lemon
1 teaspoon garlic salt

Combine all ingredients in a large bowl and toss. Refrigerate for several hours, or overnight to marinate. Serves 4-6.

Waldorf Chicken Salad
(serves 4-6)

2-3 cooked large chicken breasts (boiled or grilled), or one Rotisserie chicken cut into chunks
1 cup brown rice, cooked (may use regular or minute variety)
1 cup seedless red grapes
1 granny smith apple, diced
1 cup diced celery
1/2 cup reduced fat mayonnaise, vegannaise, or plain almond or coconut yogurt
1/4 teaspoon ground ginger
1/2 teaspoon ground cinnamon
juice from 1/2 lemon

Squeeze lemon over diced apple and mix. Combine apple with other ingredients and stir in mayonnaise, yogurt and spices until well-blended. Serve over fresh lettuce leaves and garnish with fruit.

Purple Cabbage and Granny Smith Apple Slaw

1/2 half head of purple cabbage, shredded
3 large Granny Smith Apples with peel, chopped
1 cup grated carrot
1/2 cup chopped walnuts
1/2 cup currants or raisins
1/3 cup cider vinegar
1/4 cup olive oil
2 Tablespoons (or less) agave syrup
1/4 teaspoon ginger
1/2 teaspoon cinnamon

half the juice of one lemon-toss the apple in lemon right after chopping to prevent browning. Toss cabbage, apple, carrot, walnuts and raisins together. In a separate bowl whisk vinaigrette ingredients together, pour over slaw, mix and serve. This is beautiful and tasty.

Kale Salad

1 medium bunch kale, stems removed, rinsed torn in small pieces
1/2 cup dried cranberries
1/3 cup pine nuts
Juice of two lemons
1/3 cup olive oil
salt and pepper to taste

Toss all dry ingredients together. Whisk lemon, olive oil, salt and pepper together pour over kale and toss. Serve.

Raspberry Spinach Salad

8 cups spinach, rinsed and torn into bite size pieces
1 cup raspberries
3 kiwi's peeled and sliced
1/2 cup sliced almonds
Dressing:
2 tablespoons raspberry vinegar
2 tablespoons raspberry jam
1 teaspoon agave syrup
1/3 cup canola oil

Assemble salad ingredients in large bowl. Mix dressing until well-blended. Drizzle dressing on salad and toss. Serves 6.

Orange Asparagus Salad

2 small cans mandarin oranges, drain and reserve 2 tablespoons juice
1 tablespoon canola oil
6 cup asparagus, cut in 2" pieces (about 2 pounds)
1 clove garlic, chopped
1/2 cup sliced almonds
1/2 teaspoon dark sesame oil
2 tablespoons sesame seeds, toasted
romaine or green leaf lettuce leaves

Heat canola oil in a skillet over medium heat. Add asparagus, garlic and almonds and sauté about 5 minutes. Remove from pan. Pour sesame oil over asparagus and mix well. Cool to room temperature. Stir in sesame seeds, juice and oranges. Serve on lettuce leaves. Serves 6 to 8. (Excellent as a side dish as well, just leave off the lettuce leaves).

Mandarin Salad

6 cups salad greens
1/2 cup sliced almonds
1 cup chopped celery
1 green onion, chopped
1-11 ounce can mandarin oranges, drained (reserve 1 tablespoon juice for dressing)
Dressing:
1/4 cup canola oil
2 tablespoons sugar
2 tablespoon rice vinegar
1/2 teaspoon salt
1 tablespoon chopped parsley

Mix salad greens, almonds, celery, green onion and oranges together. In a separate small bowl whisk together dressing ingredients until well-blended. Pour dressing over salad and toss to coat. Serves 4-6.

Palm Salad

12 cups mixed salad greens
1-14 ounce can hearts of palm, diced
1-4 ounce can of sliced black olives
2 cups grape or cherry tomatoes, rinsed and halved
Dressing:
1/3 cup olive oil
3 tablespoons red wine vinegar
1/2 teaspoon salt
1/4 teaspoon oregano
1 teaspoon minced garlic

Toss salad ingredients together in a large bowl. Combine dressing ingredients and whisk, or shake to blend. Drizzle dressing over salad and toss. Serves 8.

Shrimp Tostada Salad

1 pound medium cooked shrimp, tails removed
1 tablespoon olive oil
1 teaspoon sesame oil
1 teaspoon garlic, minced
1 teaspoon cumin
1 teaspoon jalapeno, seeded minced (to taste)
1 15-ounce can black beans, drained and rinsed
2 & 1/2 cups roma tomato, chopped
2 ears fresh corn, kernels cut from cobs
1 cup green onion, chopped
1/2 cup cilantro, chopped
1 head iceberg lettuce, torn or shredded
Dressing:
1/4 cup canola oil
1/2 cup lime juice with pulp
1 tablespoon white vinegar
1 teaspoon ground cumin
1/2 teaspoon salt
1/2 teaspoon garlic, minced
tortilla chips and cilantro for garnish

Heat olive and sesame oils in a large skillet over medium high heat. Add shrimp, garlic, cumin, jalapeno and corn, and sauté until warmed thoroughly about 5 to 7 minutes. Remove from heat. When mixture is cool, add black beans, tomato, green onion and cilantro.

Blend dressing ingredients together in a small bowl. Arrange lettuce on plates, with tortilla chips around edges. Pour dressing over shrimp/black bean mixture and toss to coat. Spoon evenly over lettuce on plates. Garnish and serve.

Pesto Pasta Salad

1/4 cup pesto (page 51)
8 ounces cooked rotini or corkscrew shaped pasta
1 cup broccoli florets
1 cup cherry or grape tomatoes, halved
1 jar marinated artichoke hearts, drained and quartered
1 4-ounce can sliced black olives
1 4-ounce jar button mushrooms, drained

Mix all ingredients except pesto in large bowl. Stir in pesto and toss to coat. Season to taste with salt and pepper. Chill and serve.

Cabbage Salad

1/2 head green cabbage, sliced (you can also use a bag of broccoli slaw)
1/2 cup sliced almonds
2 green onions, chopped
2 packages ramen style noodles, crumbled
Dressing:
3 tablespoons canola oil
2 tablespoons sugar
3 tablespoons rice vinegar
2 tablespoons sesame seeds
salt and pepper

Toss first 4 ingredients in a large bowl. Place all dressing ingredients in an air-tight container and shake to blend. Pour dressing over salad and toss to coat. Let marinate in refrigerator 2 hours before serving.

Marinated Vegetable Salad

1 bunch broccoli, rinsed and separated into florets
1 small head cauliflower, rinsed and separated into florets
2 cups cherry or grape tomatoes, rinsed and halved
1 4 ounce jar button mushrooms, drained
2 cups carrots, sliced
2 stalks celery, sliced
1-15 ounce can black olives, drained
1 cups bottled italian dressing

Mix all ingredients together in a large bowl. Pour italian dressing over and toss to coat. Refrigerate and marinate for 2 hours, then serve. Makes a large quantity and keeps for up to a week.

Bulgar Salad with Dried Cranberries

1 cup bulgar wheat (can substitute brown rice, farro, or barley cooked until tender)
2 celery stalks, diced
1 cup dried cranberries
1/2 to 1 cup parsley, chopped fine
juice of 1 small navel orange plus 1 tablespoon orange zest
1/4 cup olive oil

Pour 2 cups boiling water over bulgar wheat in a medium bowl, let stand 20-25 minutes until water is absorbed. Add celery, onion, dried cranberries, and parsley to bulgar wheat. In another small bowl whisk olive oil, orange juice, and zest, then pour mixture over salad. toss ingredients to coat, salt and pepper to taste.

This is yummy as a bowl with diced chicken.

Hoppin' John Salad

1 15 ounce can black eyed peas
fresh corn off 2 cobs
1/2 small diced red bell pepper
1 small yellow onion, diced
2 large handfuls baby spinach
1 chile in adobo sauce, diced
1-2 teaspoons of adobo to taste
olive oil
salt and pepper to taste

In a large skillet heat oil (about 2 tablespoons) over medium heat, when oil is hot add onion, corn and bell pepper, sauté over high heat until corn is a bit charred and onion and bell pepper are soft. Turn heat to medium and add spinach, replace the lid on the skillet and let spinach wilt, then stir to mix.

Add peas, diced adobo chile and chile sauce. Stir over medium heat until all ingredients are combined and mixture is heated thoroughly.

This salad is good served warm over brown rice, or along side grilled meat.

Roasted Potato Salad

1 bag baby red potatoes, quartered
1 bag baby mixed lettuce
2 shallots, minced
1 teaspoon minced garlic
1 teaspoon smoked paprika
2 tablespoons olive oil
salt and pepper to taste

Preheat oven to 375 degrees. Combine potatoes, shallot, garlic, and olive oil in a large bowl. Toss ingredients to coat, then spread out on a baking sheet lined with non-stick aluminum foil, sprinkle with smoked paprika, salt and pepper, and roast for 40-45 minutes, check with fork to assure tenderness.

While potatoes are still warm, spoon over baby lettuce tossed in Dijon Vinaigrette, recipe following. Enjoy.

Dijon Vinaigrette

1/4 cup olive oil
1 teaspoon dijon style mustard
juice of one lemon
Whisk all ingredients together, salt and pepper to taste.

SOUPS

Vegetarian Chili

2 tablespoons olive oil
1 cup onion, chopped
1/2 cup green pepper, chopped
3 large cloves garlic, minced
2 teaspoons chile powder
1 teaspoon oregano
1 24-ounce can V-8 juice (may use spicy or regular)
1 4-ounce can chopped green chiles
1 16-ounce can kidney beans
1 16-ounce can pinto beans
1 4-ounce can chopped black olives
1/3 cup bulgur wheat

Heat olive oil in a large non-stick saucepan over medium-high heat. Sauté onion and green pepper until tender. Add garlic and sauté two to three additional minutes. Turn off heat and stir in chile powder and oregano. Add V-8 juice and bulgar wheat and heat to boil. Then reduce heat, cover, and simmer for 20 minutes. Add beans, chiles, and olives and simmer an additional 20 minutes.

White Chili

3 15-ounce cans great northern white beans, undrained
4 large chicken breasts (sautéed or grilled), cut into bite-sized pieces, or 1 rotisserie chicken, skinned and cut into bite-sized pieces.
2 tablespoons olive oil
1 large onion, chopped
3 cloves garlic, chopped
1 teaspoon chile powder
1 teaspoon cumin
2 teaspoons oregano
2 4-ounce cans chopped green chiles
6 cups chicken broth

In a large saucepan over medium-high heat, sauté onion and garlic until onion is tender. Reduce heat and add green chiles, spices and oregano. Add chicken broth, beans and chicken and simmer for 20-30 minutes. Salt and pepper to taste.

Chicken Chowder

2 tablespoon olive oil
1 cup chopped onion
1 cup chopped red bell pepper
2 garlic cloves, chopped
5 cups chicken broth
3 cup diced red potatoes
2 & 1/2 cups whole kernel corn
1 & 1/2 cups enriched coconut milk (unsweetened)
1/3 cup all-purpose flour
1 store bought rotisserie chicken, skinned, meat cut off, and cubed
1/2 to 1 teaspoon red pepper flakes
salt and pepper to taste
1/2 cup crumbled bacon
1/2 cup sliced green onions

Heat olive oil over medium high heat in large saucepan. Sauté onion, red pepper and garlic for 5 minutes, reduce heat and add chicken broth. Add potatoes and simmer 20 minutes or until potatoes are tender, add corn and chicken. In a small bowl whisk flour and milk together until well-blended, pour into broth while stirring constantly. Simmer soup over medium heat 15-20 minutes or until slightly thickened, stirring frequently. Add salt and pepper to taste. Top with crumbled bacon (turkey or other), and sliced onions and serve.

Sweet Potato and Apple Soup

1 teaspoon olive oil
1 onion, chopped
3 cloves garlic, chopped
3 cup chicken broth
2 large sweet potatoes, peeled and chopped
2 large granny smith apples, peeled, seeded and chopped
1 & 1/2 cup enriched "milk" (coconut milk is good with this soup)
1/2 teaspoon cinnamon

Heat oil in a large saucepan on medium high heat. Add onion and garlic and sauté until tender; about 5 minutes. Add chicken broth and bring to a boil. Add sweet potatoes and apples to chicken broth, reduce to medium heat, cover and simmer until sweet potatoes and apples are tender; about 25 minutes.

Puree sweet potato and apple mixture until slightly chunky, working in small batches, then return mixture to saucepan. Stir in "milk" and cinnamon. Season with salt and pepper, and serve. Serves 6.

Thai-Spiced Coconut Corn Curry

2 tablespoons olive oil
1/2 cup chopped green onions
2 teaspoons minced garlic
1 medium red or orange bell pepper chopped
1 bag of frozen corn (I love Trader Joe's roasted corn, frozen)
2 cans coconut milk (lite or regular)
1 cup water
2 teaspoons curry powder
1/2 to 1 cup cilantro chopped

Heat oil in a dutch oven, or heavy soup pot over med high heat. Sauté garlic until lightly browned, then add onions and bell pepper, sauté for a few more minutes. Reduce heat and stir in curry powder. Add coconut milk and water slowly while stirring constantly. Stir in corn. Let simmer for 20 to 30 minutes, add cilantro just before serving, salt and pepper to taste.

Chicken Noodle Soup

1 rotisserie chicken, skin removed, chicken cut in bite sized pieces
1 cup celery, chopped
1 cup carrots, chopped
1 cup sliced mushrooms, fresh or canned
1 cup onion, chopped
2 cloves garlic, chopped
2 tablespoons olive oil
1/4 cup parsley (dried or fresh)
1 package frozen egg noodles
6 cups chicken broth
salt and pepper to taste

Heat oil In large saucepan on medium high heat. Add onion, garlic and celery and sauté 5 minutes, add mushrooms and sauté another 5 minutes. Stir in carrots and parsley. Add chicken broth to mixture and bring to a boil. Stir in egg noodles, cover and simmer on reduced heat until noodles are tender (15-20 minutes). Add chicken and heat thoroughly. Salt and pepper to taste and serve.

Beef Barley Soup

4 tablespoons margarine
1 to 1 and 1/2 pounds stew meat
1 teaspoon garlic, chopped
1 yellow onion, chopped
1 cup mushrooms, sliced
2 medium carrots, peeled and sliced
1/3 cup parsley, chopped
8 cups beef broth
1 cup barley
salt and pepper to taste

In a large stockpot, melt margarine and then sauté garlic and onion over medium high heat, about 5 minutes. Add stew meat and stir until browned. Add mushrooms and continue to sauté another 5 minutes. Add carrots and parsley and sauté for an additional 5 minutes. Pour beef broth over mixture and heat to a boil. Add barley and reduce heat to simmer. Simmer, while covered, until barley is tender, about 45 minutes. Salt and pepper to taste and serve.

MAIN COURSES

Broccoli, Orange Chicken bowls

4 cups green cabbage shredded (can use cole slaw mix)
2 cups broccoli florets, chopped
1/2 cup grated carrot
1/2 cup sliced green onions
1 large can mandarin oranges in light juice, drain and reserve juice
1/2 cup sliced almonds, toasted
crunchy Chinese noodles (thin soba noodles are good)
Dressing:
juice of one lime,
1/2 cup mandarin juice
1/3 cup rice vinegar
2 tablespoons dark agave nectar
1 teaspoon minced garlic
1/2 teaspoon minced ginger root
1 Rotisserie chicken, diced.

Toss all vegetables and fruit together in a large bowl, pour dressing over and toss with 2 cups diced chicken (Rotisserie style is easiest). This recipe is also good stir fry style over Jasmine rice. Crumble noodles and almonds on top.

Chicken Primavera Fettuccine with Lemon Garlic Sauce

10-12 fresh chicken tenders
1 cup julienne sliced carrots
1 cup julienne sliced zucchini
1/2 cup yellow bell pepper, sliced thin
1 cup sliced mushrooms
12 ounces spinach fettuccine
1 teaspoon seasoning salt
1 tablespoon margarine
cooking spray
Sauce:
2 tablespoons margarine
1 teaspoon minced garlic
1 cup chicken broth
1 cup enriched "milk"
2 tablespoons flour
juice of 1 lemon

1/4 cup chopped parsleyHeat a medium non-stick skillet over medium high heat. Add chicken tenders, sprinkle over seasoning salt, and sauté until cooked through and lightly browned.

Remove chicken and drain on paper towels. Melt 1 tablespoon margarine in skillet and add garlic, sauté over medium high heat until slightly browned. Then add vegetables and mushrooms and stir fry until slightly tender, about 5 to 6 minutes. Set aside.

Bring water to boil in a large pot. Add pasta when water is boiling and cook to desired tenderness. Drain.

In a medium saucepan melt remaining margarine. In a separate small bowl blend flour and "milk." Add chicken broth and "milk"/flour mixture to the melted margarine and heat over medium high. While stirring constantly, bring mixture to a boil. Boil 1 minute, then remove from heat. Stir in lemon juice and parsley.

In large pot, combine pasta, chicken, vegetables and sauce and toss to coat. Serve immediately.

Spinach Fettuccine with Sun-dried Tomatoes

12 ounces dry spinach fettuccine
1 cup chicken broth
1/2 cup enriched "milk"
2 tablespoons flour
1 6-ounce jar marinated artichoke hearts, drained and marinade reserved
1/2 cup boiling water
1 cup sun-dried tomatoes (dry, not packed in oil)
2 green onions chopped
salt and pepper

Boil a large pot of water and cook pasta until tender. Place sun-dried tomatoes in a small bowl and pour in boiling water, let sit while pasta cooks. In a medium saucepan over medium heat, add artichoke marinade and chicken broth. Bring to a boil for 2 to 3 minutes, reduce heat and add "milk" and whisk in flour until smooth. Cook over medium high heat until sauce begins to boil, while stirring constantly. Remove from heat and set aside.

Drain excess water off tomatoes. Mix tomatoes, artichokes and green onion into sauce and stir over medium heat until heated through. Drain pasta then return it to large pot, pour sauce over top and toss. Season with salt and pepper and serve. 4 servings

Goulash

1 pound of lean ground beef, browned
2 cans fire roasted diced tomatoes
1 package of pasta, large macaroni or shells
While browning the beef, set a large pot of water on high to boil, add a pinch of salt. Once water is on a rapid boil, add pasta, cook until tender and drain. In large pasta pot mix ground beef and diced tomatoes. Warm, and enjoy.

My mother made this dish a lot when we were kids, but of course she made it with her own home-grown canned tomatoes; it is still a favorite comfort food for me.

Creamy Chicken Noodle Bake

1 rotisserie chicken, skinned and cut into bite-sized chunks
2 tablespoons margarine
1 teaspoon garlic, minced
1/2 cup onion, chopped
1 cup zucchini, chopped
1 cup mushrooms, sliced (fresh or canned)
1/2 cup flour
2 cups enriched "milk"
1 & 1/2 cup chicken broth
1 teaspoon salt
8 ounces egg noodles
2 tablespoons margarine
1 cup breadcrumbs (Rotella)
1 teaspoon seasoning salt
all-vegetable cooking spray

In a large saucepan, melt margarine, then sauté garlic, onion, zucchini and mushrooms until slightly tender. Set aside. Whisk 1 cup "milk" with flour in a medium saucepan, until smooth. Set heat on medium high and add remaining milk and chicken broth. Stir until mixture thickens and just starts to boil, add salt and remove from heat.

Cook egg noodles in a large pot of boiling water until just tender. Drain and then return to saucepan. Mix in chicken, onion and zucchini mixture, mushrooms and white sauce. Pour into a 13 x 9 inch casserole dish, coated with cooking spray.

In a small skillet, melt margarine and sauté breadcrumbs for 2 minutes over medium high heat. Stir in seasoning salt. Sprinkle over top of casserole. Bake at 375 degrees, until casserole bubbles and breadcrumbs are golden brown. Let set for 10 to 15 minutes and serve.

Shrimp and Parsley Pasta

1 pound cooked medium shrimp, detailed
12 ounces spaghetti, or linguine pasta
1 cup chicken broth.
1 tablespoon cornstarch
2 tablespoons margarine
1/2 teaspoon chopped garlic
1 tablespoon chopped parsley
juice of 1/2 lemon

Place a large saucepan full of water on high heat. In a large skillet, heat margarine on medium high heat until melted. Add garlic and sauté until lightly browned. Add shrimp and sauté until heated thoroughly (about 5 minutes), then turn heat to low.

When water is boiling add pasta and stir. Reduce heat to medium and keep pasta boiling.

Combine broth and cornstarch in a small bowl, whisk or blend to mix thoroughly. Then pour broth and cornstarch mixture over the shrimp mixture and increase heat to medium, stirring constantly. Continue stirring mixture over medium-high heat until it thickens then reduce heat to low. Add lemon juice and parsley.

Check pasta for desired tenderness and drain. Pour pasta into a large (preferably warmed) serving bowl. Pour shrimp mixture over the pasta and toss, serve immediately. Serves 4-6.

Calzones

Filling:
1 pound fresh lean ground beef
1 26-ounce jar pasta sauce with green and black olives
1 15-ounce can artichoke hearts, quartered
Dough:
1 cup lukewarm water
1 teaspoon honey or sugar
1 tablespoon active dry yeast
2 & 1/2 cups all-purpose flour, plus extra flour for working the dough
1/2 teaspoon salt
all-vegetable cooking spray

Mix the water and honey/sugar in a medium mixing bowl. Sprinkle the yeast on top and set aside until bubbles appear on the surface. Mix the flour and salt together in the bowl of a food processor. Gradually drizzle in the yeast mixture while the processor is on. Continue to process until a ball forms. If the dough is too sticky, add a little more flour and process or knead in.

Turn out the ball of dough into a large mixing bowl coated with cooking spray, coat the top of the dough with a thin layer of cooking spray, cover and let raise until doubled in size. While dough is rising, brown the ground beef in a large skillet, then drain. Add pasta sauce and artichoke hearts, mix well.

Preheat oven to 375 degrees.

Remove dough and place on a floured work surface. Divide in 4 equal pieces.

Roll each out to approximately 1/2 inch thick rounds.

Spoon the sauce and ground beef mixture into the center of each piece of dough, about 3/4 to 1 cup in each (you may have some sauce and ground beef mixture left—it's great over pasta!) Fold over the edge of the dough and crimp edges together. Spray top of dough with a light coating of cooking spray.

Bake for 15-20 minutes, or until golden brown. Let set for 5-10 minutes and serve.

It is certainly much easier to make this recipe with already prepared dough, but the commercial brands are full of milk and/or soy protein. Trader Joe's sells pizza dough that is milk free and if you live in Omaha, you can buy it at Rotella's bakery outlet store ready to go. Just bring the dough to room temperature before working with it.

Chicken Cacciatore

10 to 12 fresh chicken tenders
1 26-ounce jar pasta sauce with mushrooms and black olives
1 15-ounce can artichoke hearts, drained and quartered
1 12-ounce package pasta, spaghetti or rotini
cooking spray

Bring a large saucepan of water to a rapid boil. Add pasta and cook until tender.

Once the water is on for the pasta, sauté chicken in a pan coated with cooking spray, until golden brown and cooked through. Add pasta sauce and artichoke hearts to chicken.

Pour cooked pasta into a 13 x 9 inch pan coated with cooking spray and cover with sauce and chicken mixture. Heat in oven at 300 degrees until warmed through and serve.

Note: this dish may be made as a casserole, as above, or you may arrange the cooked pasta onto plates and spoon the chicken and sauce mixture over top, then serve immediately.

Broccoli Chicken

10-12 chicken tenders
1 teaspoon garlic, minced
2 cups broccoli florets
1 cup slant cut carrots
1 recipe clear chicken gravy (page 113)

In a large skillet, stir fry chicken and garlic over medium high heat until cooked through. Add broccoli and stir fry until it is deep green in color and slightly tender. Reduce heat to low and add clear chicken gravy. Simmer 10 minutes. Serve over steamed rice or noodles. Season to taste with salt and pepper.

Lemon Chicken

2 tablespoons margarine
1 tablespoon olive oil
salt and pepper
4 boneless chicken breasts
2 teaspoons garlic, minced
1 cup chicken broth
1/4 cup lemon juice
lemon for garnish
fresh parsley, chopped

In a large skillet with high sides, melt margarine and add oil, heat over high heat. Add garlic and chicken, season chicken with salt and pepper, sauté until browned on both sides, then simmer until cooked through. I love the flavor that the chicken broth and lemon juice add to the chicken, but if you would like a thicker sauce, in a small bowl whisk 1 tablespoon cornstarch into the lemon before adding the broth and whisk both until smooth.

Reduce heat to medium low and add chicken broth and lemon juice. Cover skillet and simmer until chicken is cooked through, about 5 to 7 minutes. Remove cover and let simmer another 5 minutes. Serve with sauce spooned over chicken. Garnish with lemon slices and sprinkle with fresh parsley. Great with pasta or rice.

Chicken and Vegetable Stir Fry

10 to 12 chicken tenders
1 teaspoon garlic, minced
2 tablespoons dark sesame oil, divided
2 carrots, sliced
2 stalks celery, sliced
2 cups broccoli florets
1 cup sliced mushrooms
2 green onions, sliced
1 red or yellow pepper, sliced
1 cup chicken broth
2 tablespoons cornstarch
3 cups cooked rice

In a large skillet over medium high heat, sauté chicken tenders and garlic in 1 tablespoon sesame oil until cooked through. Add other tablespoon sesame oil and vegetables and stir fry until vegetables are semi-tender and bright in color. In a small bowl whisk chicken broth and cornstarch together. Reduce heat to medium and pour chicken broth mixture over chicken and vegetables and cook until thickened, while stirring constantly. Serve over rice.

Beef Tips over Parsley Noodles

1 large yellow onion, chopped
1 cup sliced mushrooms
4 tablespoons margarine
1 cup flour
1 teaspoon salt
3 pounds sirloin tips
2 cups beef broth

In a large skillet with high sides, melt margarine over medium high heat. Sauté onions and mushrooms until tender, about 5 minutes. Remove onions and mushrooms from skillet with a slotted spoon, leaving as much of the leftover juices and margarine in the skillet.

Mix flour and salt together in a medium-sized bowl. Dredge stew meat in flour mixture until well coated, then sauté in skillet over medium high heat until edges of meat are browned. Add beef broth to meat and simmer over low heat for 20 to 25 minutes until beef is cooked through and tender. Add mushrooms and onion and heat thoroughly. Salt and pepper to taste. Serves 6.

Serve over buttered parsley noodles (12 ounces egg noodles, cooked, and while noodles are still hot mix in 2 tablespoons margarine and 1/4 cup parsley).

Potato Cakes with Garlic and Onion

2 pounds red potatoes, washed and not peeled
2 teaspoons garlic, chopped
2 green onions, chopped
1 tablespoon fresh parsley, chopped
2 tablespoons yellow cornmeal, plus extra for coating cakes before frying
2 tablespoons margarine
2 tablespoons enriched rice milk
1 egg, or egg substitute, beaten
2 tablespoons olive oil for frying

Boil potatoes in a large pot of water until tender, rinse, drain, and cool. Return potatoes to pot, add garlic, margarine and rice milk and mash. Stir in green onion, parsley, 2 tablespoons cornmeal, salt and pepper to taste. Cover and refrigerate until well-chilled, 2 to 4 hours.

Form potato mixture into small cakes, dip in beaten egg, coat with cornmeal. Fry in a medium skillet with olive oil over medium high heat until heated through and golden brown on each side.

May also bake these cakes: Preheat oven to 425 degrees, line a baking sheet with foil and brush with olive oil and place cakes on pan. Bake for 10 minutes on each side, until golden brown and heated through.

Garlic Mashed Potatoes

2 pounds red potatoes, peeled and quartered
2 14-ounce cans chicken broth
2 tablespoons margarine
2 teaspoons garlic, minced
salt and pepper

In a medium saucepan bring broth to a boil, add potatoes and reduce heat, simmering until potatoes are tender. Drain potatoes, reserving 1/2 cup broth. In a small skillet melt margarine, then sauté garlic over medium high heat until golden brown. Pour garlic and margarine over potatoes in a large bowl, add chicken broth and mash. Salt and pepper to taste and serve.

Wild Rice Casserole

1 small box wild rice (11-12 ounces)
1 can stewed or fire roasted tomatoes
2 cups chicken broth
1/2 cup sliced green olives
1/4 cup dried toasted onion bits

Bring broth to a boil in a medium saucepan, add rice, when at at rapid boil, turn down to a simmer and place the lid on. Once rice is fully cooked, most of the broth should be absorbed, then add tomatoes, olives and onion, stir together and place mixture in a small casserole coated with cooking spray.

Bake in a 350 degree oven until warm and bubbly, you may need a bit more broth if the mixture is too dry.

Potato and Zucchini Gratin

3 medium potatoes, thinly sliced (russet or yukon)
1 medium zucchini, thinly sliced
2 teaspoons seasoning salt
2 tablespoons margarine
1/2 cup onion, chopped
1 & 1/2 cups enriched "milk"
2 tablespoons flour
1/4 teaspoon nutmeg
all-vegetable cooking spray

Coat a 8 x 8 inch casserole with cooking spray. Arrange 1/3 of the potatoes over the bottom of the casserole, sprinkle lightly with seasoning salt. Layer 1/2 of the zucchini on top of the potatoes and again sprinkle with seasoning salt. Repeat layering and sprinkling the potatoes and zucchini ending with the potatoes on top. Set aside.

In a medium saucepan heat the margarine over medium heat to melt. Add the chopped onion and sauté until onion is tender. In a separate small bowl, whisk or blend "milk" and flour until it is smooth, pour into the saucepan with the onion and bring to a boil over medium heat while stirring constantly. Remove from heat once sauce just begins to boil. Stir in nutmeg.

Pour the white sauce over the potatoes and zucchini and bake. Cover with foil and bake for 40 minutes at 350 degrees. Uncover and bake 10 to 15 minutes more, until golden brown.

Good on it's own, but if you want a crust on top, toast 1 cup of bread crumbs in a small skillet on medium high heat, then melt in 3 tablespoons margarine and sauté until bread crumbs are thoroughly coated. Just prior to baking the gratin, sprinkle the bread crumb mixture over the potatoes and zucchini. the result will be a "buttery" golden crunch on top.

Spinach and Rice Gratin

1 cup dry white or brown rice
1 & 1/2 cups chicken broth
1 10-ounce package frozen chopped spinach, thawed and squeezed dry
2 tablespoons margarine
1/2 cup onion, chopped
1/2 teaspoon minced garlic
1 cup mushrooms, sliced
1 cup enriched rice milk
2 tablespoons flour
1/2 cup egg substitute
1 teaspoon salt
1/2 teaspoon pepper
all-vegetable cooking spray

In a medium saucepan, bring chicken broth to a boil. Add rice, reduce to simmer, and cover until rice is tender, about 35 minutes.

In a medium skillet melt margarine, then sauté onion and garlic until onion is tender, about 5 minutes. Add mushrooms and continue to sauté for 5 minutes. In a large bowl, mix together spinach, and onion\mushroom mixture. Mix in rice. In a separate small bowl whisk together rice milk, flour and egg substitute. Pour over rice mixture and stir to blend.

(Insert breadcrumbs from the previous recipe for a nice golden crunch.)

Pour into a 13 x 9 inch casserole coated with cooking spray. Bake, uncovered, at 350 degrees until set, and light golden brown, 35-45 minutes.

Red Beans and Rice

4 cups cooked white rice
2 tablespoons olive oil
1 medium onion, chopped
1 teaspoon garlic, minced
3 15-ounce cans kidney beans, undrained
1 & 1/2 cups chicken broth
1-2 teaspoons cajun seasoning, to taste
(A bit of turkey pepperoni is good here too.)

Heat oil in a large skillet with high sides. Sauté onion and garlic over medium high heat until onion is tender and golden brown. Pour in kidney beans, chicken broth and seasoning. Cover and simmer, over reduced heat for 50 minutes to an hour. Spoon over rice and serve. Serves 4-6.

GRAVY AND SAUCES

Chicken Gravy

2 tablespoons margarine
2 cups chicken broth
3 tablespoons flour
salt and pepper to taste

Melt margarine in a medium saucepan. Add 1 cup chicken broth to 2 tablespoons flour and blend until smooth (or may be shaken to mix in an airtight container). Into the saucepan over medium heat add remaining 1 cup chicken broth and flour\chicken broth mixture. Stir constantly while mixture heats and just begins to boil. Remove from heat. Season to taste with salt and pepper. Serve.

*This recipe can be made substituting vegetable, beef, fish stock or turkey broth as well.

Clear Chicken Gravy, or **Glaze**

2 tablespoons margarine
2 cups chicken broth
2 tablespoons cornstarch
dash salt

Melt the margarine in a medium saucepan. Combine 1 cup chicken broth with cornstarch and blend until smooth. Pour remaining cup chicken broth and broth and cornstarch mixture into the saucepan. Over medium heat, cook until mixture just begins to boil, while stirring constantly. Remove from heat. Season with salt to taste.

Mushroom Gravy

1/2 pound fresh mushrooms, sliced
2 tablespoons margarine
1/2 teaspoon minced garlic
2 cups beef broth
2 tablespoons cornstarch

Over medium heat in a non-stick skillet, sauté the mushrooms and garlic in margarine. Combine the beef broth and cornstarch in a small bowl and blend, or whisk until smooth. Pour the beef broth and cornstarch mixture into a medium saucepan placed over medium heat and stir until the mixture begins to boil. Remove from heat and add mushrooms and garlic. Season with salt and pepper to taste.

Basic White Sauce (Bechamel)

2 tablespoons margarine
2 cups enriched unflavored unsweetened almond milk*
3 tablespoons flour
salt and pepper

Melt margarine in a medium saucepan. Combine almond milk and flour and blend until smooth. Pour almond milk\flour mixture into saucepan and increase heat to medium. Stir constantly until mixture just begins to boil. Remove from heat. Salt and pepper to taste.

*I like using the almond milk in this recipe, it is thicker than rice milk and doesn't add any coconut flavor as the coconut milk does. When making sauces with thickener, allow mixture to boil only briefly (one minute or so) and then remove from heat. The sauce will keep a thicker consistency.

Lemon Dill Sauce

1 recipe basic white sauce
1/8 cup fresh dill, chopped
juice of 1/2 lemon

Prepare basic white sauce and whisk in lemon and dill. Season with salt to taste. This sauce is good over fish.

Pesto is great over pasta, or spread lightly on bread and grilled. Most Pesto recipes contain parmesan cheese, these are lighter and milk-free.

Basil Pesto

1 cup fresh basil leaves
3 garlic cloves, peeled
1/4 cup pine nuts
1/4 cup fresh lemon juice
1/8 cup olive oil

Place all ingredients in a food processor or blender. Process until mixture becomes a smooth paste. Makes 1/2 cup. Use 1/4 cup over 8 ounces of pasta. Pesto freezes well in ice cube trays, use one frozen cube for a basic pasta recipe.

Cilantro Pesto

1 cup fresh cilantro
3 garlic cloves, peeled
1/4 cup walnuts
1/8 cup fresh lemon juice
1/8 cup olive oil

Place all ingredients in a food processor or blender. Process until mixture becomes a smooth paste. Makes 1/2 cup.

MEATLESS DISHES

Black Bean Burgers

3 15-ounce cans black beans, undrained
3 cups cooked brown rice
1 medium onion, diced
1 chipotle pepper in adobo sauce, dice
1-2 teaspoons adobo sauce from chiles in adobo
2 teaspoons chopped garlic
1 tablespoon olive oil
1 teaspoon chile powder
1 teaspoon salt
1 & 1/2 cups bread crumbs
3 tablespoons minced cilantro
Olive oil or all-vegetable cooking spray for frying

Heat oil in a large skillet on medium high heat. Add garlic and onion and sauté until onion is softened, about 5 minutes. In a large food processor, process rice and beans until blended, but not fully pureed, about 1 minute, then add chipotle pepper and sauce, pulse to mix. Place bean mixture into a large bowl. Add onion, garlic, chile powder and salt and stir until blended. Stir in bread crumbs and cilantro.

Shape bean mixture into patties and fry until in a small amount olive oil or cooking spray. Serve hot. Serve burgers as you would hamburgers. These burgers freeze well if you wrap them individually and then store them in an airtight container. Makes 12 large burgers.

BBQ Baked Bean Burgers

3 15-ounce cans vegetarian baked beans, undrained
3 cups cooked brown rice
1 medium onion, chopped
2 teaspoons chopped garlic
2 tablespoons olive oil
2 tablespoons barbeque sauce (I like hickory or mesquite flavor)
1 teaspoon salt
3 cups bread crumbs
Olive oil or cooking spray for frying

Heat oil in a medium skillet over medium high heat. Sauté onion and garlic until onion is softened, about 5 minutes.

In a large food processor, process rice and-beans until blended, but not smooth. Add onion and garlic, salt, and barbeque sauce until just blended. Place bean mixture in a large mixing bowl.

Add bread crumbs to bean mixture and blend. Depending on dryness, you may want to add a bit more BBQ sauce or olive oil.

Shape bean mixture into patties and fry until golden brown. Serve as you would hamburgers. Makes 12 large burgers.

Brown Rice Burgers

2 cups mushrooms, sliced
1 cup celery, chopped
1 & 1/2 cup carrots, chopped
1 large onion, chopped
2 tablespoons garlic, chopped
1/2 stick margarine
2 cubes chicken bouillon
1/3 cup boiling water
2 teaspoons Lawry's seasoning salt
4 cups cooked brown rice
2 eggs
1/2 cup Malt O'Meal cereal, uncooked

Heat olive oil in a large skillet over medium high heat. Add garlic and onion, and sauté until just browned. Add mushrooms, celery and carrots and sauté until softened. Cool mixture. When cooled, puree mixture in food processor until mixture appears grated, but still some chunks remain. Set aside. In a large bowl mix rice with 2 beaten eggs. In a separate small bowl, mix boiling water and bouillon cubes and stir until dissolved. Add bouillon mixture and seasoning salt to the rice mixture and stir to blend, then add vegetable mixture and mix well. Let stand for 15 minutes.

Heat a large non-stick skillet to medium heat. Form the rice mixture into burger-sized patties and brown on each side, Serve with hamburger buns, lettuce, tomato, pickle, onion and other condiments. Makes 18-20 burgers.

Roasted Vegetable Burgers with Brown Rice and Lentils

3 cups water
2 chicken or vegetable bouillon cubes
3/4 cup brown rice
1/2 cup brown lentils, rinsed and drained
1/3 cup cracked wheat
1/2 cup roasted red peppers, chopped
1/2 cup green onion, chopped
1 cup sliced mushrooms
1 teaspoon chopped garlic
1 tablespoon olive oil
1 tablespoon oregano

2 eggs
1/2 cup flour
salt and pepper
all-vegetable cooking spray

Bring water to a boil in a medium saucepan. Add bouillon, rice, lentils and cracked wheat. Stir to dissolve and mix in bouillon, cover, and reduce heat to low. Cook 40 to 45 minutes, until tender. Remove from heat and cool.

In a heavy skillet, heat olive oil over medium heat. Add garlic and sauté until light golden brown. Add mushrooms, peppers, and green onion and sauté 5 to 6 minutes. Remove from heat and stir in oregano, cool.

When above mixtures are cool, stir together in a medium large bowl. Season to taste with salt and pepper. Mix in eggs and flour. Form mixture into patties and turn a heavy skillet coated with cooking spray. Cook patties 3 to 4 minutes on each side until golden brown in color,

Serve burgers as you would hamburgers. I like these with barbeque sauce.

Pinto Bean and Potato Burritos

10 large (10-inch round) flour tortillas
2-15 & 1/2 ounce cans vegetarian refried pinto beans
3 medium baking potatoes
1 small can chopped green chiles
2 medium green onions, chopped
seasoning salt or salt free seasoning
all-vegetable cooking spray
salsa

Pierce potatoes several times with a fork, then microwave the potatoes 10 minutes on high stopping at five minutes to turn potatoes a quarter turn. Set potatoes aside and let them cool. Meanwhile in a medium-sized heavy saucepan heat the refried beans on low heat. When the potatoes are cool enough to handle, dice into 1/2 inch pieces. Place a large skillet on the stove with the range turned onto medium high heat. Once the skillet is hot, spray the skillet well with cooking spray and add onions and potatoes. Sauté the onion-potato mixture on medium heat until the potatoes are golden brown. Season, stir and remove from heat.

Fold the potatoes into the beans and stir to blend. Fill each of the flour tortillas with approximately 1 cup of the bean and potato mixture, wrap, add salsa and serve. You may also garnish the burritos with fresh tomato, black olives, shredded lettuce, or guacamole. You may want to microwave each plate quickly before serving, so they stay warm.

Black Bean and Sweet Potato Enchiladas

1 16 ounce can commercially prepared enchilada sauce (I like the green chile sauces best on these enchiladas)
1-2 tablespoons olive oil
1 small yellow onion, diced
2 teaspoons minced garlic
1/2 teaspoon cumin
1 pound sweet potatoes, peeled and diced
1 can diced fire roasted tomatoes
1 cup cilantro minced
1 can (15 ounce) black beans, drained and rinsed
1 jar green salsa
1/2 cup water
12 corn tortillas

In a large skillet heat oil, add onion, garlic and cumin and sauté until soft and fragrant. Add sweet potatoes and 1/2 cup water, bring to a boil and cover to steam sweet potatoes. Once sweet potatoes are soft, add tomatoes, salsa, cilantro and black beans, stir over medium heat until thoroughly warmed and

incorporated; it doesn't matter if mixture mashes a bit.
Preheat oven to 350 degrees. Warm corn tortillas so they are easier to work with. Fill tortillas and roll up, placing seam side down in a 13 x 9 inch casserole coated with cooking spray.
Pour sauce over top of enchiladas and bake for 10-15 minutes until warmed.
Garnish with avocado, guacamole, cilantro, lime and corn tortilla chips.

DESSERTS: COOKIES, CAKES, AND COMFORT FOODS

Monster Cookies

1 & 1/2 cup brown sugar
1 stick margarine
1 cup peanut butter
3 eggs
1 & 1/2 cup flour
1 cup sugar
2 teaspoons baking soda
1/2 teaspoon salt
2 teaspoons vanilla
4 cups rolled oats
6 ounces semi-sweet chocolate chips, or chocolate chunks

Cream first 3 ingredients together then add eggs, one at a time beating after each addition. Mix in sugar, flour, baking soda, salt and vanilla. Stir in rolled oats, then chocolate. Spoon dough onto cookie sheets in heaping tablespoons. Bake at 350 degrees for 10-12 minutes. Cookies should be light brown. Remove pan from oven and let cookies sit on pan for an additional 2 minutes before removing.

**May add chopped nuts, raisins or cinnamon raisins, as you wish. These cookies freeze well in an airtight container for at least one month. Freezing them the same day as you bake them keeps them very fresh and chewy. They thaw quickly when removed one at a time for snacking! These are my most favorite cookie!

Chocolate Chocolate-Chip Walnut Cookies

1/2 stick margarine
2/3 cup packed brown sugar
2 eggs
2/3 cup all-purpose flour
1/4 teaspoon baking powder
1 teaspoon vanilla
1/4 teaspoon salt
1 12-ounce package semi-sweet chocolate chips, divided
1 cup chopped walnuts

Preheat to 350 degrees. Place 6 ounces chocolate chips in a microwave-safe bowl and cook on high for 1 to 2 minutes, until chocolate is melted, stopping to stir every 30 seconds. Mix melted chocolate together with margarine, brown sugar, eggs and vanilla. Mix in flour, baking powder and salt. Stir in remaining chocolate chips and walnuts.

Drop cookies onto a cookie sheet by teaspoonfuls. Bake 11 to 12 minutes or until puffed and set.

Cool on cookie sheet for 2 minutes then remove and cool.

Peanut Butter Chip Cookies

1 cup creamy peanut butter
3/4 cup brown sugar
2 large eggs
1 teaspoon baking soda
1 teaspoon vanilla extract
1/2 teaspoon salt
2/3 cup oats
3/4 cup dark chocolate chips

Preheat oven to 350 degrees. Mix together Peanut butter and brown sugar, then add eggs one at a time beating after each addition. Mix in baking soda, vanilla and salt, then stir in oats, until well-blended. Last mix in chocolate chips.

drop onto cookie sheets a couple inches apart and bake for 8-10 minutes until just barely browned. Let cool and enjoy.

Cranberry Orange Oatmeal Cookies

2 sticks margarine, softened
1 cup sugar
1 cup packed brown sugar
2 eggs
1 teaspoon vanilla
1 tablespoon orange zest, grated
2 cups all-purpose flour
1 teaspoon baking soda
1/2 teaspoon salt
3 cups rolled oats

**2 cups dried cranberries

Preheat oven to 350 degrees. Mix together margarine and sugars until smooth, then add eggs, and blend thoroughly. Mix in vanilla and orange zest. In a separate bowl, mix flour, baking soda and salt together. Add flour mixture to the dough and stir until well blended. Stir in oats, and cranberries. Drop by teaspoonfuls onto cookie sheets and bake 10-12 minutes until light golden brown. Leave cookies to cool on pan for 2 minutes then remove to a wire rack.

**You may substitute diced dates or prunes (I love the orange scented prunes in these cookies),or other diced dried fruit. Raisins, cinnamon raisins or chocolate chips are also great. (When adding chocolate chips you may take out the orange zest, or leave it in for a great flavor treat!)

Oatmeal Chip Cookies

2 sticks margarine, softened
1 cup sugar
1 cup packed brown sugar
1 egg
2 teaspoons vanilla
2 cups all-purpose flour
1 teaspoon baking soda
1/2 teaspoon salt
1 teaspoon cinnamon
1/4 teaspoon nutmeg
3 cups rolled oats
1 12-ounce package chocolate chips

Preheat oven to 375 degrees. Cream margarine and sugars until creamy and smooth. Mix in egg and vanilla. Add flour, salt, soda and spices and mix thoroughly. Stir in oats and chocolate chips. Drop by rounded teaspoons onto cookie sheets and bake 9-10 minutes. Cool 2 minutes on cookie sheets. Makes 4-5 dozen cookies. Store in airtight containers or freeze after cooling for longer freshness.

Ginger Cream Cookies

1 & 1/2 sticks margarine, softened
2 cups sugar, plus extra sugar for rolling cookies
1/2 cup molasses
2 eggs
2 teaspoons vanilla extract
4 cups all-purpose flour
4 teaspoons baking soda
1 teaspoon salt
1 teaspoon ground ginger
2 teaspoons ground cinnamon
1/4 teaspoon ground nutmeg
1 teaspoon ground cloves

Preheat oven to 350 degrees. Cream together margarine and sugar. Mix in molasses, eggs and vanilla until well blended. Mix in flour, baking soda, salt, and spices. Roll dough into 1-inch balls (can be frozen at this point) and then roll in sugar. Bake for 8 to 10 minutes, until cookies are flat and have a cracked appearance. Cool and frost. Makes about 5 dozen cookies.

Frosting:
2 tablespoons margarine, softened
2 cups powdered sugar
1 teaspoon vanilla
2-3 tablespoons enriched "milk"
red food coloring

Combine first 3 ingredients and mix until smooth. Add 2 tablespoons milk and mix well, if frosting is too stiff, add more milk. Add a drop or two of red food coloring if desired, so the frosting becomes light pink in color. I entered these in a cookie contest at the hospital once, one of the judges said they were "too sweet." Never knew that could happen!

Snickerdoodles

2 sticks margarine, softened
1 & 1/2 cups sugar
2 eggs
3 & 1/4 cups flour
2 teaspoons cream of tartar
1 teaspoon baking soda
1/2 teaspoon salt
1/2 cup sugar and 3 tablespoons cinnamon for garnish

Cream margarine, and sugar together. Add eggs, one at a time, and beat after each addition. Mix dry ingredients (flour, cream of tartar, baking soda and salt) into batter. Chill dough about an hour. In a small bowl mix together sugar and cinnamon. Roll dough into small (1-inch) balls and roll in sugar and cinnamon. Bake until very lightly browned, about 10 to 12 minutes in an oven preheated to 400 degrees. Cookies will puff up slightly and then flatten down.

Pecan Snowballs

2 sticks margarine, softened
1/2 cup sugar
2 teaspoons vanilla
1 teaspoon salt
2 cups all-purpose flour
1 cup finely chopped pecans (a mini food processor works great)
powdered sugar for rolling

Cream margarine and sugar together. Mix in vanilla, then mix in salt and flour. Once dough is well blended, mix in pecans. Roll into small (1-inch) balls and bake in a 325 degree oven for 20 minutes. When first removed from the oven roll in powdered sugar when cool enough too touch, wait 15-20 minutes and roll them again.

Peanut Blossom Cookies

1 stick margarine, softened
1/2 cup sugar
1/2 cup brown sugar, packed
1/2 cup peanut butter
1 egg
1 teaspoon vanilla
1 teaspoon baking soda
1 teaspoon salt
2 & 1/4 cups all-purpose flour
sugar for garnish
large semi-sweet chocolate chips for garnish, optional, since they do not make milk-free Kisses, the dark chocolate chunks from Whole Foods, 365 brand work nicely.

Cream together margarine, sugars, and peanut butter. Add egg, beating well. Mix in vanilla, flour, baking soda and salt. Roll dough into 1-inch balls, (may need to chill dough first), then roll in sugar. Bake in an oven heated to 375 degrees for 10 minutes. Remove cookies from oven and decorate immediately with chocolate. Cool on pan 2 minutes, then remove.

Cocoa Krinkle Cookies

2 sticks margarine, softened
1 & 1/3 cups sugar
2 eggs
1/2 cup cocoa powder
1 teaspoon vanilla
3 cups all-purpose flour
2 teaspoons cream of tartar
1 teaspoon baking soda
1/2 teaspoon salt
powdered sugar for garnish

Cream together margarine and sugar, then add eggs, one at a time, beating after each addition. Mix in cocoa and vanilla until well-blended, then mix in flour, cream of tartar, baking soda and salt. Chill dough for 1 hour. Preheat oven to 375 degrees. Roll dough into 1-inch balls, then rollin powdered sugar and bake for 10 to 12 minutes, or until slightly firm when tapped. Cool on cookie sheets for 2 minutes, then remove.

A quicker way to make them? Yes, with a brownie mix.

Brownie Mix Krinkles

1 package brownie mix for 13 x 9 inch pan, or Devil's food Mix
1/3 cup vegetable oil
2 eggs
1 teaspoon vanilla
powdered sugar

Heat oven to 350 degrees. Mix all ingredients together until thick dough forms. refrigerate dough for 20-30 minutes for easier handling. Roll into 1 inch balls and roll each in powdered sugar. Place on cookie sheet and bake 8-10 minutes until puffed, but not browned. Cool for 2 minutes and remove from cookie sheet.

Crunchy Fudge Cookies

1 box brownie mix
3 cups cinnamon coated cereal
1/3 cup water
1 egg
2 teaspoons vanilla
1/2 cup mini chocolate chips

Preheat oven to 350 degrees. Mix all ingredients together except the cereal, once it is well mixed, add the cereal and stir to coat. Drop by spoonfuls onto cookie sheet. Bake 10 minutes. These are really good and <u>very easy</u>. Go Big Red!!

Macaroons

1 14-ounce package flaked coconut
3/4 cup sugar
1/2 cup all purpose flour
1/2 teaspoon salt
4 large egg whites
1 teaspoon almond extract
1 teaspoon vanilla extract

Mix coconut, sugar, flour, and salt in a medium mixing bowl. In a separate bowl, lightly beat egg whites, and then stir into coconut mixture. Blend well. Mix in almond and vanilla extracts. Drop by rounded teaspoonfuls onto cookie sheets. In an oven preheated to 325 degrees, bake for 20 minutes or until cookies are light golden brown. Remove from cookie sheets and cool on wire racks. Makes approximately 2 dozen.

Option: Mix in 1 cup of mini semi-sweet chocolate chips before baking, pecans are also good.

Almond Meringues ("Dead Man's Bones")

2 large egg whites
1 cup sugar
1 cup all-purpose flour
1 teaspoon vanilla
1/2 teaspoon almond flavoring
1 cup slivered almonds

Beat egg whites until stiff, then add sugar and continue beating until it is well incorporated. Fold in flour. Stir in vanilla and almond flavorings and slivered almonds. Drop in rounded teaspoons onto cookie sheet lined with parchment paper. Bake in an oven preheated to 350 degrees for 10 to 12 minutes. Cool completely, then carefully remove cookies from waxed paper.

Chocolate Meringues

3 large egg whites
1 cup sugar
3 tablespoons cocoa powder
2 tablespoons flour
1 teaspoon vanilla extract

Preheat oven to 325 degrees. Beat egg whites until frothy, add sugar slowly until all sugar is beaten in and mixture is stiff. Fold in cocoa, flour and vanilla. Line cookie sheets with parchment paper. Drop in rounded teaspoons onto cookie sheets, or you may use a piping or decorating bag fitted with a star tip, and press out 1-inch stars. Bake for 14 to 16 minutes, let cool completely then carefully remove cookies from waxed paper.

Mocha Meringues

3 large egg whites
1 cup sugar
2 tablespoons cocoa powder
1/2 tablespoon instant coffee granules
2 tablespoons flour
1 teaspoon vanilla extract

Beat egg whites until frothy, then add sugar gradually until incorporated and mixture is stiff. Fold in cocoa, coffee granules, flour and vanilla. Drop by teaspoons onto cookie sheets lined with parchment paper and bake in an oven preheated to 325 degrees for 14 to 16 minutes. Cool completely, then carefully remove cookies from waxed paper.

Fudge Brownies

4 ounces semi-sweet chocolate chips, or chopped semi-sweet chocolate bars
1 & 1/2 sticks margarine
1 cup sugar
1 cup brown sugar
3 eggs, beaten
1 teaspoon vanilla
1 cup all-purpose flour
1/2 cup walnuts, optional
all-vegetable cooking spray

Preheat oven to 350 degrees. In a small microwave-safe bowl, melt chocolate chips and margarine on high for 1 minute. Remove from microwave and stir, if chocolate chips are not all melted, return to microwave for another 30 seconds, remove and stir. Place sugars in a large mixing bowl and pour chocolate mixture over top. Mix or stir until sugar is well incorporated. Beat in eggs. Mix in vanilla, flour, and nuts. Pour into 13 x 9-inch baking pan coated with cooking spray. Bake for 30 to 35 minutes until a toothpick comes out clean.
Makes 20 to 24 brownies.

Peanut Butter Brownies

1 stick margarine, softened
1 cup creamy peanut butter
1 cup brown sugar
1/2 cup sugar
2 eggs
1/3 cup enriched "milk" or canola oil
1 teaspoon vanilla
3 cups all-purpose flour
1 & 1/2 teaspoons baking powder
1/2 teaspoon salt
6 ounces semi-sweet chocolate chips, optional
all-vegetable cooking spray

Cream margarine, peanut butter and sugars together. Beat in eggs, one at a time. Mix in milk and vanilla. Stir in flour, baking powder and salt. Stir in 4 ounces chocolate chips. Spread batter into a 13 x 9-inch baking pan coated with cooking spray. Sprinkle remaining chocolate chips evenly over top. Bake in an oven preheated to 350 degrees for 20 to 25 minutes or until golden brown on top. Makes about 2 dozen brownies.

Rocky Road Brownies

1 stick margarine, softened
1 cup sugar
2 eggs
1 teaspoon vanilla extract
1/3 cup cocoa (unsweetened)
1 & 1/2 cups all-purpose flour
1 teaspoon baking soda
1/4 teaspoon salt
1 cup mini-marshmallows
1/2 cup semi-sweet chocolate chips
1/ 2 cup chopped walnuts or slivered almonds
all-vegetable cooking spray

Preheat oven to 350 degrees. Cream margarine and sugar together. Beat in eggs. Mix in vanilla, cocoa, flour, baking soda and salt. Pour batter into a 9 x 9-inch baking pan coated with cooking spray. Bake for 25 minutes. Sprinkle marshmallows, chocolate chips and walnuts/almonds evenly over top of batter and return to oven for 5 more minutes. These are easier to cut after they have been chilled.

Lemon Bars

Crust:
1/2 cup sugar
6 tablespoons margarine, softened
1 & 3/4 cups all-purpose flour
Filling:
5 eggs
1 & 1/2 cups sugar
1 tablespoon grated lemon rind
1/2 cup fresh lemon juice
5 tablespoons all-purpose flour
1 teaspoon baking powder
1/4 teaspoon salt
powdered sugar for garnish

Preheat oven to 350 degrees. Mix first three ingredients together until mixture is crumbly (a food processor works well for this). Press mixture into the bottom of a 13 x 9 inch pan and bake for 15 to 18 minutes, may be very lightly browned. Cool.

Beat eggs with an electric mixer until foamy and lemon colored. Add sugar and beat well. Then add lemon rind, lemon juice, flour, baking powder and salt. Beat until well-blended. Pour lemon mixture over crust and bake at 350 degrees for 20 to 25 minutes, until set. Cool, then sprinkle powdered sugar. Makes 20-24 bars.

Caramel Orange Bread Pudding

1 tablespoon grated orange zest
1/2 cup orange juice
1/3 cup sugar
4 eggs
2 cups enriched rice milk
1/2 cup brown sugar
2 teaspoons vanilla extract
1/2 teaspoon cinnamon
1/8 teaspoon nutmeg
12-1 inch thick slices of french or sourdough bread (baguette style)
all-vegetable cooking spray
Topping:
3 tablespoons brown sugar
1/2 teaspoon cinnamon
1 tablespoon margarine
1/4 cup Coconut Creamer

Combine first three ingredients in a small saucepan. Bring to a boil over medium heat, stirring constantly. Boil until mixture is thickened slightly, about 6-8 minutes, remove from heat stir in coconut creamer and set aside.

Whisk eggs until well blended. Whisk in rice milk, vanilla, cinnamon and nutmeg. Arrange bread slices in a 13 x 9 inch pan coated with cooking spray. Pour cooled orange mixture over the bread, then pour egg mixture over bread. Cover and chill in refrigerator for 1-2 hours, or overnight. Preheat oven to 350 degrees. Mix together ingredients for topping until crumbly and sprinkle over top of pudding. Bake for 40 to 45 minutes until golden brown and puffed up. Serve warm, garnish with fresh fruit.

Rice Pudding

1 cup white rice
2 cups "milk" plus 1 cup reserved
1/2 cups sugar
2 tablespoons margarine
2 teaspoons ground cinnamon
2 teaspoons vanilla
2 egg yolks
1/2 cup raisins

Combine milk, rice, sugar, margarine, and cinnamon in a large saucepan. Cook over medium heat until rice is tender and creamy, stirring frequently. Remove from heat and stir in vanilla and raisins. In a small sauce pan heat remaining 1 cup milk, whisk in egg yolks and cook an additional 2 minutes. Mix egg mixture into rice mixture stirring constantly until well-mixed, then and simmer to desired consistency. May be served warm or cold.

Cinnamon Raisin Bread Pudding

8 cups cinnamon raisin bread, cubed
8 eggs, may use egg substitute
1 & 1/2 cups sugar
1/2 cup brown sugar
2 cups enriched "milk"
2 teaspoons vanilla
1/2 teaspoon cinnamon
all-vegetable cooking spray

Preheat oven to 350. Spray a 9 x 13 inch pan with cooking spray. Place bread cubes in pan. Whisk together eggs, rice milk, sugars, vanilla and cinnamon. Pour egg mixture over bread, let sit for 15-20 minutes. Place pan in a larger pan filled with 1 inch of water. Bake for 35 to 40 minutes, until puffed and lightly browned. Serve warm.

Vanilla Cinnamon Pudding

1/4 cup sugar
1 egg
2 cups enriched vanilla "milk"
4 tablespoons Tapioca (small size)
1/2 teaspoon ground cinnamon

Whisk above ingredients together in a heavy saucepan over medium-high heat. Continue heating, while stirring constantly, until mixture boils. Remove from heat and cool. Pudding may be served warm or chilled.

This pudding is great spooned over fresh fruit, such as strawberries!

Banana Bread Pudding

2 & 1/2 cups enriched "milk"
1/2 cup sugar
1 teaspoon cinnamon
1/2 teaspoon nutmeg
3 eggs, beaten
1/2 cup brown sugar
2 tablespoons margarine
2 ripe bananas, sliced
4 cups french bread, cubed
all-vegetable cooking spray

Preheat oven to 350 degrees. Whisk milk, eggs, sugar, vanilla, cinnamon and nutmeg until blended. Add bread and let stand 10-15 minutes.

In a medium skillet heat margarine and brown sugar. Continue stirring until mixture boils and sugar is dissolved. Add sliced bananas and coat in brown sugar mixture, stirring constantly, 1-2 minutes. Fold bananas into bread mixture and pour into an 8 x 8 inch baking dish coated with cooking spray.

Bake for 45-50 minutes, until pudding is golden brown and set. Serve warm with coconut or almond creamer.

Blueberry "Cobbler"

1 large loaf french, or sourdough bread, crusts trimmed and cubed
6 eggs
1 cup enriched "milk"
1/2 cup sugar
1/2 cup brown sugar
2 tablespoons cornstarch
1 teaspoon cinnamon
8 cups blueberries (may be fresh or frozen)
all-vegetable cooking spray

Place cubed bread in a large mixing bowl. In a separate large bowl, whisk together eggs and rice milk. Pour over bread mixture to coat, cover and refrigerate for several hours or overnight.

When ready to bake, mix sugars, cornstarch and cinnamon in a large mixing bowl. Toss in blueberries to coat. Pour blueberries into a 13 x 9 inch baking dish coated with cooking spray, top with soaked bread cubes.

Bake in an oven preheated to 375 degrees for 30 to 40 minutes. Serve on a platter inverted, or spoon out, serves 8.

Chocolate Chip Zucchini Cake

2 & 1/4 cups all-purpose flour
1/2 cup unsweetened cocoa
1 teaspoon baking soda
1 teaspoon salt
1 stick margarine, softened
1/4 cup canola oil
1 small jar/container baby food prunes
2 eggs (egg substitute may be used)
1 teaspoon vanilla
1/2 cup enriched dark chocolate almond milk
2 cups grated zucchini, fine
6 ounces (1 cup) semi-sweet chocolate chips
1/2 cup chopped walnuts
all-vegetable cooking spray

Preheat oven to 325 degrees. Spray a 13 x 9 inch pan with cooking spray. Mix flour, cocoa, baking soda and salt together in a medium mixing bowl and set aside. Beat margarine, sugar, oil, and prunes until well blended. Add eggs one at a time, beating well after each addition. Mix in dry ingredients alternately with chocolate milk. Beat in vanilla. Stir in grated zucchini until just mixed. Pour batter into prepared pan. Sprinkle chocolate chips and nuts over top. Bake 45-50 minutes until a tester comes out clean. May be served warm or cooled. Great with almond or coconut milk "ice cream."

German Chocolate Cake

1/2 cup margarine, softened
4 ounces semi-sweet chocolate chips
1 & 1/2 cups sugar
1/2 cup enriched dark chocolate milk
2 large eggs
2 & 1/2 cups all-purpose flour
2 teaspoons baking powder
1/4 teaspoon salt
all-vegetable cooking spray

Preheat oven to 350 degrees. Melt margarine and chocolate in a mlcrowave-safe bowl on medium high until melted, about 1 & 1/2 minutes. Stir until all chocolate is melted. Mix in sugar and vanilla, then beat in eggs one at a time. Mix in baking powder and salt, then mix in flour in small amounts alternating with milk. Blend well. Pour into a 13 x 9 inch baking pan coated with cooking spray. Bake at 350 degrees for 30 minutes, or until a wooden toothpick inserted in the center comes out clean.

Frosting:
1 cup sugar
1/2 cup brown sugar
2 tablespoons cornstarch
1 & 1/2 cups enriched "milk"
4 tablespoons margarine
1/3 cup flaked sweetened coconut

Mix together sugars and cornstarch in a heavy saucepan. Turn range on to medium heat and whisk in milk. Add margarine. Bring to a boil over medium heat and cook for 1 minute, stirring constantly. Remove from heat, add pecans and coconut. Spread over cake while still warm and serve.

Cherry Coffee Cake

1& 1/2 cups flour (plus 2 tablespoons)
1/2 cup sugar
1/2 teaspoon salt
1/2 teaspoon baking powder
1/4 teaspoon baking soda

1/2 stick margarine
1 egg
3/4 cups enriched "milk"
1 teaspoon vanilla
1 cup frozen
tart cherries, chopped
all-vegetable cooking spray

Preheat oven to 350. Mix dry ingredients together in a large bowl. Add margarine and cut into flour mixture until crumbly. Whisk egg, vanilla and milk together in a small bowl and add to flour mixture and stir or mix until smooth. Coat frozen cherries in 2 tablespoons flour and add to batter, stirring just until incorporated. Pour into 13 x 9 pan coated with cooking spray. Sprinkle with streusel and bake for 45-50 minutes until a toothpick inserted comes out clean, and top is golden brown.

Streusel mix:
1/4 cup brown sugar
2 tablespoons flour
1/4 teaspoon salt
1/4 teaspoon cinnamon
1/4 teaspoon nutmeg
2 tablespoons margarine
1/4 cup rolled oats
1/2 cup sliced almonds

Mix above ingredients together until well blended and crumbly.

Cinnamon Coffee Cake

1 & 3/4 cups sugar, divided
1/2 cup chopped walnuts
1 tablespoon ground cinnamon
1 tablespoon unsweetened cocoa
3 cups all-purpose flour
1 tablespoon baking powder
1/2 teaspoon salt
1 & 1/2 sticks margarine
4 eggs
2 teaspoons vanilla extract
1 cup enriched "milk"
all-vegetable cooking spray

Preheat oven to 350 degrees. Spray a 10 inch tube pan with cooking spray. Mix 1/2 cup sugar, walnuts, cinnamon and cocoa and set aside. Mix flour, baking powder and salt in a large bowl. Beat margarine with an electric mixer until smooth. Beat in remaining sugar. Add eggs, one at a time, beating well after each addition. Add vanilla. Mix in dry ingredients alternately with milk until mixture is well blended. Spoon 1/3 of the batter into the pan, then sprinkle 1/2 of the walnut mixture on top. Pour remaining batter in the pan and sprinkle with remaining walnut mixture. With a knife, cut through the batter to swirl in the walnut mixture. Bake for 45-50 minutes, until tester comes out clean. Cool. Loosen cake with knife around the edges of the pan before inverting onto plate.

Peach Upside-Down Cake

2 peaches, sliced, (about 16 slices)
1 tablespoon margarine, melted
1/2 cup packed brown sugar
2 tablespoons chopped walnuts
1 & 1/4 cups all-purpose flour
1/3 cup rolled oats
1 teaspoon cinnamon
1/2 teaspoon ginger
2/3 cup granulated sugar
3/4 teaspoon baking powder
1/2 teaspoon baking soda
1/4 teaspoon salt
4 tablespoons margarine, softened
1 large egg
1 teaspoon vanilla
1/2 cup enriched "milk"

Preheat oven to 350 degrees. Coat the bottom of a 9-inch round cake pan with melted margarine, sprinkle brown sugar and walnuts over top of margarine. Arrange peach slices over top of brown sugar and walnut mixture. Set aside. Combine flour, oats, cinnamon, ginger, sugar, baking powder, soda and salt in a medium bowl. Mix in margarine, beat in egg, then stir in vanilla and milk until batter is smooth. Pour into prepared pan and bake for 30 to 35 minutes or until a toothpick comes out clean. Allow cake to cool in pan for 5 to 10 minutes then loosen edges and invert.

Chocolate-Dipped Banana Bits (frozen)

2 cups dark chocolate chips
1 Tablespoon coconut oil
chopped salted peanuts, coconut flakes, peanut butter for roll ins and toppings
2-3 ripe bananas cut in 1 inch pieces

Freeze sliced bananas on a cookie sheet for 20-30 minutes while melting chocolate and coconut oil in a microwave safe bowl, stopping every minute to stir, until melted.

Dip each banana slice into chocolate to coat, then let excess chocolate drip off and dip into toppings, and place onto wax paper lined tray. Once dipped bananas are on tray, dollop a bit of creamy peanut butter on tip if desired. Freeze again for 1-2 hours, then serve, or eat one at a time until all gone

Apple Cake with Salted Caramel Sauce

4 cups diced apples, mixed, some tart, some sweet, peel can be left on
1 lemon, quartered
3 cups all-purpose flour
1 and 1/4 cups sugar
1/2 cup brown sugar, packed
2 teaspoons pumpkin pie spice
1 teaspoon cinnamon
1/2 teaspoon baking soda
2 teaspoons baking powder
1/2 teaspoon salt
1/2 cup coconut oil, soft, not melted
3 large eggs
1 container coconut milk yogurt, plain
1/2 cup coconut milk
1 tablespoon vanilla extract
zest and juice of one orange

Preheat oven to 350 degrees and prepare a tube or bundt pan with margarine or cooking spray. Dice apples and place in bowl, squeeze lemon juice over apples as you dice, so they will not brown. Place flour into large bowl, mix in sugars, spices, baking soda, powder and salt. Cut in coconut oil until flour is fine and crumbly.

In a smaller bowl whisk eggs until light yellow, and well-blended, mix in coconut yogurt, coconut milk, vanilla, juice and zest.

Pour wet mixture into flour and stir until blended, batter will be thick. Add apples. pour evenly into tube or bundt pan. Bake at 350 degrees for 45-50 minutes until puffy and browned, remove when tester is inserted and comes out clean. I like this cake really moist so, I turn off the oven at about 45 minutes and leave cake in, then take out when still warm after about 15 minutes.

Cool the cake for 10-15 minutes further and then loosen sides with a knife and invert on plate. Enjoy!

I had all these apples, leftover
Granny Smith, Jazz, Pink Lady,
Fuji, needed to do something with them . . . so I made cake.
Warm, gooey, moist and delicious,
Cake.

I just love fall!

Salted Caramel Sauce

3/4 cup brown sugar
2 tablespoons corn syrup, or maple syrup
2 tablespoons water
1/4 to 1/2 cup coconut milk creamer
1/2 to 3/4 teaspoon kosher salt

Stir sugar, syrup and water together in small saucepan, and bring to a boil over medium heat. Continue to stir occasionally until thick and brown colored (10 to 15 minutes). Remove pan from heat, gradually add the creamer to caramel mixture, and stir to incorporate. Add salt 1/4 teaspoon at a time—you certainly do not want it too salty. Drizzle caramel over warm apple cake and enjoy.